A ROOTED JOURNEY HOME

A Taste Of ~~His~~ *Her* -Story…
The Present Learns From The Past

SIERRA CLARK

First published by Ultimate World Publishing 2022
Copyright © 202 Sierra Clark

ISBN

Paperback: 978-1-922714-87-9
Ebook: 978-1-922714-88-6

Sierra Clark has asserted her rights under the Copyright, Designs and Patents Act 1988 to be identified as the author of this work. The information in this book is based on the author's experiences and opinions. The publisher specifically disclaims responsibility for any adverse consequences which may result from use of the information contained herein. Permission to use information has been sought by the author. Any breaches will be rectified in further editions of the book.

All rights reserved. No part of this publication may be reproduced, stored in or introduced into a retrieval system, or transmitted in any form, or by any means (electronic, mechanical, photocopying, recording or otherwise) without the prior written permission of the author. Any person who does any unauthorized act in relation to this publication may be liable to criminal prosecution and civil claims for damages. Enquiries should be made through the publisher.

Cover design: Ultimate World Publishing
Layout and typesetting: Ultimate World Publishing
Editor: Rebecca Low

Ultimate World Publishing
Diamond Creek,
Victoria Australia 3089
www.writeabook.com.au

DEDICATIONS

To my four♣︎ heartbeats I wasn't brave enough to meet. To every black child knowing who they are, who they really are!

To the embellishment of systemic racism and every life taken. To not being judged by the color of their skin, but instead, by the content of their character.

To being the example, the change you want to see. Dare to dream out loud.

To no longer needing hashtags like #QuisForLifeInc #LoveNotBlood #NotMySon #BlackLivesMatter and #CancerSucks. To Black Wall Street Part II.

To the Hugh D. Burgess estate, Laurel Park, Red's Snack Shack, The Tomlinson Adult Learning Center, Jordan Park, The Deuces, The Historic Manhattan Casino.

To the freedom bells that have yet to ring, to the unheard cries of our ancestors whose scarred and unscarred backs are now the hills that support us.

To my mother, father, siblings and all my fill-in-the-blank people. And last but not least, to my life's legacy, tribe, and generational wealth.

CONTENTS

Dedications	iii
Foreword	vii
Introduction	1
Chapter 1: Big Memories	3
Chapter 2: Like Mother Like Son	13
Chapter 3: The Vail is Toren	21
Chapter 4: Inquiring Hearts Want to Know	27
Chapter 5: Generationally Cursed or Just Unlearned	37
Chapter 6: A Divided House	45
Chapter 7: No, You May Not	51
Chapter 8: Family Legacy	57
Chapter 9: Ang3ls Unaware	61
Chapter 10: Where Were You on the Night of?	67
Chapter 11: Hard Pills Can Be Swallowed	73
Chapter 12: Quantum Leaping	81
Chapter 13: Intentional Mindset	85
Chapter 14: They Can Tell By The Way I Walk, I Ain't From Around Here	93
Chapter 15: Let's Talk About Death, Can We?	107
Chapter 16: Daddy's Girl	121
About The Author	143
Speaker Bio	145
Call To Action	147

FOREWORD

History's significance and meaning have captivated us all at more points in our experience than we know. Some could say that the history you are taught could psychologically impact your thoughts and actions. Some would even say the experiences of your past blood relatives, or past lives, have an impact on who you are today, both mentally and emotionally.

History can liberate parts of your psyche that have been purposely cut off from their primary functions. Learning something as simple as an ancestor's story could raise that same energy in your DNA, and unlock that link. It may help you find out that the history that was taught to you about your ancestral timeline was full of untruths and plagiarisms. Those are eventful and altering impressions.

Begin with whatever reason you have to indulge in the curiosity of yourself and your bloodline beyond your great grandparents. We are the prophecies of old walking in the flesh but we sometimes miss that jewel of knowledge because we were taught a history that had us looking in different directions.

Those that came before our mothers and fathers, our great grandparents and even their parents. Those that were mysteriously erased from what we were taught to be history. We've all discovered monumental moments in history that were never in any history books you've read. But they are part of history.

Let no rock go unturned when looking to shine a light on those dark corners of your history or your family's history. Sometimes, things aren't always examined in the right light. An open and evolved mind will always be forced to revisit a prior judgment. It's a part of your evolutionary process, and it's a part of human history.

To re-examine the choices made before a level of maturity or enlightenment occurred or was discovered. If made more aware of this, we could focus more on the process to perfect the experience.

Your bloodline is more important in this reality than we sometimes want to keep in mind. And I say that in the mindset of the indigenous roots we continue to disregard for whatever reasons we have accepted to disown our families. Not judging, not choosing a side, just simply stating that the history of your family will always give you clarity.

History involves land and the many things that were once owned by your bloodline. We were landowners, inventors, bankers, doctors, and everything that still exists. You may not be able to learn everything about your history, but the bread crumbs are there to follow. It takes the spirit, heart, and mind to work in unison on this journey.

If you are mature enough—spiritually, mentally, and emotionally—you will be able to review and discern without judgment, but with clarity. The choices made impacted the bloodline as a whole. The people, places and things, shaped and/or created the infrastructure that is the family.

FOREWORD

Family is business. This may not make sense, but it is an element etched in our being. Your family was great at more than one point in history. Both family and humanity were impacted by the influence of your bloodline. So family is business, which is yet another reason to research your family and its infrastructure.

When researching history, there are sometimes voids in time when it comes to paper documents. Sometimes you have to put your boots on the ground and go back to your ancestral ways. Go and sit down with the elders of the family and ask those questions that no one seems to be asking.

Your motherboard (oldest woman or man in the family) has folders that no one has tried to open and read. We haven't paid attention to the cycles of our ways. Even with the devices we use to assist us in navigating throughout our day, we never truly use them at their full potential before we discard them for newer models.

We have lost the connection to our family history because many of us don't have a connection to the family and/or its legacy. We've allowed the choices of individuals to influence us to distance ourselves or even disconnect ourselves from our family.

Again, no judgment or ridicule, but choices are results. It's a hard and heavy journey, one of family and history. But it could also be rewarding, liberating, and empowering. Those are the end results we aim for, aim for with the awareness that other frequencies travel that path as well.

Sierra Clark embarked on the journey of family history in order to see the foundation that was laid down before her time arrived. This book is an insight into her discoveries of simply asking questions and listening, two things that we either forgot how to do or just simply don't care for the results those two things can produce.

When I began to interact with Sierra more, I realized that her light was different. Her personality and energy were not the same as the majority of the people in our city. So I asked her about her roots and ancestry, I was curious. She knew that her grandfather was of Belizean descent.

I myself am always encouraging those that are copper colored to research more of their family history, and the origins of the timeline that you know of. So I encouraged her to ask more questions in order to learn more about herself.

While combing through the layers of history of family, you'll discover their ties to land and cities. To counties and acres of land. You'll realize the legacy that was history was more than likely snatched away by paper genocide or genetic genocide. But there are ways to reconnect with the land and legacy. With thorough focus, you may be the one to unlock and break cycles of poverty and voids in communication and advancement within your bloodline and city.

The land is a vital piece in the contracts our ancestors had in place. From the livestock to the agriculture, it was the status quo of the times. Some families owned hundreds of acres and allowed others to rest and work peacefully while on that land. Those contracts and verbal agreements were held up by the people involved in the community. The individuals in the community were another vital piece to the overall ecosystem, an ecosystem that built and nourished countless people and families. So if nothing more than that, your family history could've been one of servitude while having ownership

I guarantee you will find knowledge of the intelligence, the bravery, the royalty, and the respected in your bloodline if you look deep and with an open mind and spirit. There is power in the name and the name is tied to the blood, so there is power in the blood.

FOREWORD

We are living in an era that is all revealing, so we are becoming all-knowing. So allow this book to encourage you, entertain you, and most of all, encompass you as you read the stories of some of Sierra's family history. May it plant a seed in you to embark on your own journey if you aren't already on the mission.

Don't be embarrassed or stifled. Don't be easily moved or emotionally weak. Don't be so attached that you may let your discoveries alter the goal. You and whomever you partner with on this mission have to be solid. There will always be opposition in any endeavor in life, but those obstacles are merely tools to sharpen you for the journey and we've had to endure some sharpening in one form or another.

Timothy Barber

INTRODUCTION

Imagine the feeling of being locked up, alone, scared, and restricted. This space is fortified, and it seems like there is no way to escape. This space, you, yourself have built, although you were unaware of that. You have been in there longer than you care to admit. This place has held you hostage for most, if not all, of your life. This haunting, uneasy feeling is no longer wanted. This disruptiveness is coming from deep within.

I now know, that going IN was the WAY out. Going in has provided so much clarity. This place that has haunted me for so long was not a physical space, it was a mindset. It hindered me, stunted my growth, and made me unable to see the power that lived in me.

How does one find their purpose? In the words of the owl on the Tootsie Pop commercial, "The world may never know." Although there is no cookie-cutter plan, nor a way to find it, one thing is for sure, you might keep getting lost and the journey may seem unrewarding and never-ending if you don't synchronize with the compass of your soul.

Going in was the means to getting out. Intentionally understanding my inner pull. So, when the waves of life come crashing and people, seasons, and things change, stay the course. Then, when the opportunity is presented, it will bring you in alignment with what lies within.

I have a motto, life should be experienced, not just lived. There is nothing final or new under the sun. Purpose is what was banging on my soul while my mind and heart kept me in a prison with no walls at all. Purpose is something we experience in real-time; it is something we uncover, then discover as we continue to move forward. As you continue to remove your limitations and break free of your complacent mindset, remember that purpose is something you choose to walk in, not something you stumble upon.

Becoming in-tune with purpose allows you to align your actions with your long-term goals. Besides, how does one know where they're going if they don't know where they've come from?

So, off I go on the rooted journey home.

Chapter 1

BIG MEMORIES

When I pulled up to my Uncle Desmond's house, joy was coming out of my ears, much like a hot kettle on the stove. My visit was a surprise, but I was so excited to learn about my grandfather. Desmond is the second born and the first person I interviewed. As I put the car in park, I looked up from the steering wheel and noticed jars and jugs outside lining the structure of the house. They were used to catch rainwater. This was a clear sign of the country boy in him. I gathered my things and got out of the car, taking it all in. I'm telling you, some days it felt like I could inhale through my fingers, and exhale from my toes. What I discovered in writing my first book is still having its way with me.

I adjusted my clothing and cleared my throat, feeling like a nervous reporter. I then knocked on the door and one of his grandchildren opened it. It was Billy, one of Constance's sons. Constance, whom we called Lucy, was my uncle's adopted daughter. (That only needed to be stated for the purpose of keeping the facts to the seeds and the lineage of my grandfather accurate.)

My uncle had no biological children, but through his second wife Desiree, our family grew. I think the last time I saw him was at his wife's surprise birthday party. "Hey, Uncle," I said as I entered the house.

He was sitting at the table in front of the television playing solitaire on a tablet. I'm not sure if I shared with him the reason for my visit, but I got right to business by asking the first question, "How was it growing up?"

Desmond - "I survived and worked and did everything I needed to do."

Sierra - "Were your sisters in school with you?"

Desmond - "I had most of them beat by a couple of years, so it was never long. I always left them."

Sierra - "Ok, so what is the order? Wanda, my momma, Patty..."

Quickly, he interrupted me and said, "It's me, then your mother!" So, he started over...

Desmond - "Wanda! ME! Duke, Patti, Chantay."

Sierra, jumping in to say it with him - "My momma, Patti and Chantay because she's the baby." I finish it off.

Sierra - "What is your full name?"

Desmond - "Desmond H. Burgess."

Oh yeah, that's right, the H is the same as my grandfather's first name, Hugh. As my excitement rose, I couldn't stop smiling. This book is so needed, for so many reasons. Getting the hang of being a reporter kicked in, lol and the questions started. Although I had come up with six questions to ask everyone, it seemed we were heading off that beaten path.

BIG MEMORIES

Sierra - "What year did you start working with the city?"

Desmond - "Way back then."

He could not give me a year and it seemed that he was having to search for his words. At the same time, something sparked in that brain of his. It was as if he went into a place in time where he could recall something. The gaze in his eyes and the look on his face screamed of everything that surrounded that moment in time. His face was saying, I remember it like it was yesterday.

He took me back in time as he had a flashback of his first paycheck. He said his first paycheck was exactly $78. I asked him if he remembered how many hours he was working back then. I thought he said 80 hours, but he said eight hours. I was thinking weekly, it was clear he was thinking daily. (Do the math.)

Sierra - "What was your job description?"

He was unable to give me an exact description, but could still recollect some details. He did manage to get out that he started working as a city sanitary worker and then got transferred to working on garbage trucks. At some point, he was promoted to driving the trucks. I asked if he had a certain route that he had in the city, but he said he was just responsible for going where he was needed and where other drivers had broken down.

Something in me was able to understand what was going on here. I looked up at him as he was moving around. It was here where I painfully noticed that my uncle was obviously suffering from either a form of dementia or Alzheimer's. But he finally got it out. "30 years," he confidently blurted. "I was working with the city for over 30 years."

Sierra - "What's your favorite memory of your father?"

Desmond - "He taught me how to maintain, survive, stay alert, and work hard."

Sierra - "If you had to describe your father, how would you describe him to me? What kind of man was he?"

Desmond - "He was very easygoing. We had a good understanding where we could talk about anything. My dad would tell me the things that I needed to do and I listened."

I asked a random question about activities that he might have done with his dad, like fishing. He then jumped to his mother so we stayed there. I learned how Grandma loved catfish and he would often go fishing for her, catching them and cleaning them. It was the cleaning part he didn't particularly like.

Sierra - "So, how old were you when you all moved to Union Street?"

He said he was about 15 or 16 years old when they moved there and still remembers being a young teenager when they did. He recalled them playing softball in the field across the street from my grandmother's house. He had this big feline smile on his face when he realized he was remembering things from his youth that he had not remembered in a while.

I inquired about how old he was when my grandparents split up because, in my earliest memories of them, they lived in two separate houses. He gave an address to a house on Royal Court, if I'm writing that correctly. I'll confirm this when I interview the others. I watched him go in and out of memory farts, I've used that terminology since I read Toni Fisk's novel #Dine With Dignity. I watched him struggle with finding his thoughts and smile at the joy that was found when rediscovering what he once already knew.

It is said that we don't forget anything, we hold onto the information until it's actually needed. After seeing this firsthand, I'm inclined to think that dementia doesn't fall under this umbrella. He then chuckled out loud…you can tell because his belly jiggled. He started sharing a memory of my mother (Duke) where they were all in the room. My mother stuck something into the socket and the force was so powerful that it knocked her backwards. He said he's not sure why in the world she would have wanted to do something like that. I agreed while guaranteeing that she learned a lesson that day and probably never did it again.

Sierra - "Were you close with your siblings or did you all used to fight all the time?"

He said things were pretty good between him and his siblings. Glancing at him, he had this look on his face. I smiled, it almost felt like when the computer says, "Downloading, please wait." I waited, still smiling. I just knew I was about to hear some tea, like catfights between sisters, or something like that. His next rebuttal switched the whole genre of the question before.

He started to talk about my grandfather's property. Although It was passed down to his kids once he died in 92, I'll probably always see it as my grandfather's! Desmond was my grandfather's only son. This was the last of what the city of St. Petersburg had on record as the Hugh Burgess Estate. Which, at one point in time, included a total of five properties. The one he was speaking of is in front of 22nd Ave South and (9thst) Martian L. King St, along the alleyway behind Atwater's Cafeteria. It saddens me to even think about this, but since he bought up the topic, let's talk about it.

> **BIOGRAPHICAL SKETCH**
> Hugh "Champ" Burgess
>
> **BORN:** August 23, 1923
> Belize, British Honduras
>
> **EDUCATION:** British Honduras Educational System
>
> **CHRISTIAN EXPERIENCE:** He was a Baptist
>
> **EMPLOYMENT:** After 25 years with the Pinellas County School System, he retired from the maintenance department in 1989
>
> **ARMED SERVICES:** During World War he served in the
>
> **DEMISE:** July 11, 1992
>
> *Survivors to remember with cherished memories ...*
>
> **TWO SONS:** Desmond Burgess & wife Desiree, and Eddie Larry & wife Juanita
>
> **FOUR DAUGHTERS:** Wanda, Eliza, and Chantay Burgess; Pattie McLeod & husband Bradford
>
> **FOUR SISTERS:** Pearl Dixon, Violet Williams, Majorie Ware, Lucille Mims
>
> **ONE BROTHER:** William Lord
>
> **11 GRANDCHILDREN:** All of St. Petersburg, FL
>
> **OTHERS:** A host of Nieces, Nephews and other Relatives and Friends

During Life

My grandfather, born in Belize, made his way to St. Petersburg. I'll get to the whos and hows later in the story but for now, let's stay on topic. This duplex built in 1948, was the last we had of the Hugh Burgess Estate. The sale date was February 27th, 1976. I'm not sure if my grandfather was the first owner or not. The land directly behind this was once a part of the estate as well. It's actually the house I have fond memories of from my childhood. Not much about it is crystal clear, more like a thick fog or haze, yet I can remember the memories created and the experiences we had at this house like it was yesterday.

I remember going to visit my grandfather here when we come down from Tarpon Springs on the weekends, spring breaks, and holidays. It was a two-story house made of red brick with a garage and a nice size front yard. I smile as I remember the time my granddad would be with all his grandkids and we would have the best of times. There was a picnic table in the far north end of the yard where the magic happened. It gave him joy to have all of us gathered around. We had the best times there, memories were made. We were always eating something, and there was always plenty of it.

My grandfather was definitely a family-oriented person. It is clear now that it was more than that! I now understand history. I was undeniably able to see just what kind of man my grandfather was. Now at 41, no longer a little girl, I was also able to understand him better. He was a man who came to America by way of a ship that docked in North Florida, Jacksonville, or Lake City, where he met my grandmother Elnora. He served this country in one of the wars. Elnora had one son, Larry. I don't know anything about his father, cannot say I have even heard a story. Yet, nonetheless, that was not an issue for Hugh and one thing led to another, then Wanda was born, and they decided to make St. Petersburg, Florida their home.

My grandfather, a black man, an immigrant, and a property owner, far away from Belize, came to the not yet segregated city of St. Petersburg. He came in the era where the dreams of Martin Luther King had not pierced the nightmares of realities for people with his skin color. You know the dream, where he says that we should be judged by content of our character, not our color.

As the color fills this page, a measure of pride came over me, parting the way for me to see why I was confronted with the feeling of, "How do I know where I'm going, if don't don't know where I come from?"

I told you that I have a strong feeling that my uncle is suffering from memory loss. However you decide to look at it, he was expressing how he moved out of the property and allowed his sisters to move in and that he did his best to maintain it to make sure that it could stay in the family.

He went on to explain the layout of the property as far as he remembered it. It was a one-bathroom, two-bedroom house. I was then trying to get some tea from him, or some juicy gossip for lack of a better word, so I asked him something and told him that he didn't have to worry about me telling anyone. I asked who his favorite sister was and he said neither one of them, he loved them all the same. I was surprised, so I asked again, "Neither one of them was your favorite?" He then swayed back to the family property and how the lack of passing down the knowledge about the legal part of owning property me and my siblings didn't know.

I had always wanted a big brother, so I had a specific idea of what having one would be like, motivating my next question. I asked whether he had to defend or fight for his sisters a lot in school and he said not at all. He expressed how all of them were fully capable of taking care of themselves when it came to fighting. He said depending on how heated things got, he would show up on the scene just to let people know and be aware that he was their big brother. "Was not no more said was not no more done," is what he said verbatim, but I totally comprehend what he was trying to say to me.

I then shared with him a story that I found out about my mom one afternoon when me and Auntie Patty decided to go to lunch and I ran into a classmate that went to school with them. He told the story of how my mother was a big tomboy and how all the guys in Bogey Ciega were afraid of her. It was so bad that the guys in the school came up with a call they would scream out in the hallway when they saw her coming so other guys would recognize that she was on her way and everybody would scatter.

Auntie Patty was younger than my mother and my uncle, so that means they would have graduated before she did. She confessed that she didn't have boyfriends in high school because all of them were afraid of my mother. She put the notice out when graduating that nobody should talk to her younger sister and this gentleman that revealed his fear of my mother confirmed that to be the 100% truth.

I changed the topic and started asking about his mother and grandmother. I asked if he remembered his grandmother's name, which is his mother's mother. He said her name was Catherine and she was married to a Hancock from his recollection. He said his grandmother was buried in the same cemetery as his mother and father. He talked about one of his memories of them visiting the graveyard looking for them.

BIG MEMORIES

His mom, dad, and mother's mother were all buried at the same cemetery. I shared with him what I heard on the news about this burial ground as they had some bad publicity lately due to some kind of financial situation they had gotten into, so they were now going under new management.

While I sat there on the edge of my seat with suspense, as if I was watching a horror picture and waiting for the killer to show up, I couldn't help but smile at myself at the idea of uncovering my family history. The idea of learning where I come from and the idea of now knowing where I'm going. The idea is that I am learning my history to find my rooted journey home.

As my uncle was flipping through the pages of his broken memory, I noticed some weights in the window. Steel, five-pound little weights, so I started doing some arm exercises while listening to him playback some of his own memories that he was reminded of. I watched that joy bubble up into a smile on his face as he said he had upgraded to the 20-pound weight and he liked that better. I mentioned to him that I was on my journey of wellness and health and that I realized you don't always have to go to the gym, you can do intentional things throughout the day to burn calories and to stay fit.

Time would have it that now when I think of a 20lb pound weight, I'll remember this moment with my uncle. I did feel a sense of urgency to disrupt the old way we were doing family. I noticed a pattern that offered no return, on a life well-lived, on healthy bonds, and communication in my family. Let the words of this next chapter be in honor of my uncle, Desmond H. Burgess, who gained his wings before the book was published.

> ***Precious moments become seeds if they're given the right environment and planted in the correct place. Like your ♥ memories, they'll bloom and last forever.***
> ***- SMC***

Chapter 2

LIKE MOTHER LIKE SON

My uncle was always known to grow hot peppers, which he learned from his mother who always kept a hot pepper tree on the porch. He said he currently had two in the back that were growing very well. I currently have a few in my freezer from when he gave me a bunch the last time I was there.

This time, I inquired about what kind of hot peppers they were and he said they were the habanero ones that the islanders use because my grandfather was an islander, that is why my grandmother grew them. He then referenced how his last batch of seeds came from his cousin Kenny. His father and Kenny's mother are siblings, but they grew up as best friends rather than cousins

He recommended I find Kenny because he would know a whole lot about my granddad, him, and Sylvia. My granddad was Kenny's favorite uncle. Sylvia was my grandfather's oldest niece (her mother) so they could definitely help me with more information on my grandfather and his siblings. He mentioned being unsure if cousin Barbara still had the house. I tried to be more direct and ask whether he was referring to the house that was down by the school. I wanted to make sure what page he was on.

I wasn't sure if he was talking about something that was being revealed from a memory or something that I didn't know. As I flipped through the pages of my own thoughts, my next question came to me and I asked, "Well, were Grandma and Grandad ever married?" He said yes and to help him recollect this memory, I brought up my grandfather living in the big brick house behind Atwater's cafeteria and my grandmother living on a dead-end on Union Street.

He said yes, they were still married, they were just separated. Then his cheekbones arose from his face and he smiled again as if he ran across one of his favorite memories. He mentioned that if his mother wanted to go out, she was going! His smile got bigger when the thought seemed to paint a picture of that exact moment, he emphasized that his mother enjoyed going out dancing. "Shaking a leg" were his exact words. I asked if he knew where she went and he said he couldn't recall the name.

I wanted to jog his memory, so I asked if she used to go to the place on 22nd Street. It was the popular place to go for things like that at the time. My cheeks were lifting from my face as a chuckle filled the air and I leaned back in my seat because I too have a thing for dancing, so to know that my grandmother made it her business to go out dancing made my heart smile. Then, I inquired about what kind of work my grandmother did. For some reason, I remember hearing that she worked as a mortician so this was my way to clarify this.

He said no, she didn't work at a funeral home, she took care of a family. The family name was Reece.

Ms. Reece's house over by Campbell Park on the brick road down around the corner. He said you go down that road like that, and then you go up a hill a little bit. I felt like he was talking about what I know as Booker's Creek. He then began to brag about this avocado tree the lady had in her yard. The avocados were as big as his head and he said he loved climbing the tree. Getting the avocados sometimes was easy because they would already be on the ground.

I told him it was funny that he would even mention avocados because, for the previous month, I had been craving avocados like crazy. I remember my grandmother eating avocados when I was younger and even when she offered, I never had a desire to taste an avocado and now I get super excited when I even think of avocados. The interesting thing about this is, that it's not a mental meaning that my brain is telling myself. It's an internal meaning speaking to my brain.

There is something on the inside of me that is craving them so much that even the thought of them makes my mouth water. I can't really explain it, I can just tell you what is happening to me at the moment and at the time that my uncle was sharing with me about this avocado tree. I realized the only thing he and I have in common with avocados is my grandmother.

As we were on the topic of this strange thing that was happening to me, I mentioned beets. He smiled, dad liked them things. I remember my grandad eating beets when I was younger and this too was something that, out of the blue, I started craving without my permission. It was so bad that I felt like I was almost being taken over when I went into the grocery store and put all these cans of beets into my grocery cart.

I didn't have any explanation for it at that moment but I could talk to my uncle. Perhaps it was just me channeling the energy of my grandparents because I wasn't even eating, I was scarfing down the two things that I remembered from my childhood. Even though I wanted nothing to do with them when I was a child, I was suddenly eating them like they were my favorite candy and the best thing in the world.

If you can let me paint a picture for you, I opened a can of beets, dumped them in a bowl, and ate them with a fork. Even as I was putting the fork up to my mouth, my brain was asking, "What are you doing to me?" while I was eating like it was the best meal I ever had.

My uncle said that he has always been a fan of vegetables. So have I. I can eat a meal and not have any meat at all as long. As you give me a plate of vegetables, I'm a happy girl. He was on a roll now and his memory of things was pouring in. He mentioned missing hog head chilli. I thought he was referring to hog head cheese that I remembered eating in a sandwich. He said it was something named hog head chilli. I guess it's safe to say it was made up of the same meat just made to look like chilli. He said his momma could cook it good and right.

So I asked him what his favorite things were that his mother used to cook. He said that upside-down pineapple cake was his favorite. He closed his eyes as if he could see it sitting there on a plate in front of him, imagining how the pineapples used to be all around it with the brown sugar dripping down. So many things were connecting just by having this conversation with my uncle, I wouldn't have believed it if it wasn't something that I already knew, but not for the sake of writing this. The truth is that upside-down pineapple cake is my favorite cake and it is the cake that I know I throw down on when I make it. After I finished licking my lips at the thought of this pineapple upside-down cake, which turns out to be both our favorite cake, I proceeded with my questions.

The next question was about the high school he graduated from. He graduated from Dixie Hollins and said they had just integrated because, at Dixie, there were only 20 to 30 black people in that school. He got training from Dixie and said shop class taught him how to throw a nail. He got carpenter skills and mentioned building what sounds like the dugout for the baseball field. I asked how *the experience of coming from an all-black school to going to an integrated school was. He said none of the children ever gave him a tough time.*

I then told him the story that my mom told me about memories. I want to say she said it was Bogie Ciega High School that she was going to. They would be leaving school and she would have to hurry because if she were found on the wrong side, the west side of 49th Street, they could be in trouble. It was a danger zone for black people to be on that side of the street. She said she remembers having to run depending on how late whatever they stayed after school ran for.

I chimed into our present moment, deep into the story. I noticed what was playing in the background the whole time. The Syfy channel. I told him how my mother loves the Syfy channel as well. Syfy and playing the pool game on the computer is all he does nowadays, he said

That jogged a memory for me. I believe it was Auntie Patty who told the story of Uncle Larry having my cousin Tony up at the pool house with him. Tony is a beast on the pool table, he has entered competitions and is still playing pool to this day. Uncle Larry was my grandmother's first child. I am unaware of who his father was but mention Uncle Larry and the vibe shifts because Larry had died just a little over two years before. I am not sure of what their relationship was before but I know that he had the privilege of living down the sidewalk from his big brother so they had opportunities to build a bond.

My uncle spoke very highly of the benefits of having his big brother live so close to him. They would visit each other every day, sit down and talk, laugh and reminisce. He reflects back on the day that he got the call from Larry's wife, Juanita. He was supposed to go down the day before but he just wasn't feeling well. He said he couldn't go and he woke up to the call from Auntie Juanita letting him know that his brother had died peacefully in his sleep that night. He said it took a while for that to even sink in, so he didn't go down there right away.

At the time of writing this book, we had also just lost Auntie Juanita, perhaps three months prior, so the two lovebirds are together again. I intentionally tried to change the subject because I could feel my uncle's and my emotions changing, so I asked if he played any sports in high school. He said he used to play basketball at 16th Street Middle School.

Desmond - "Even my sister played some kind of sports. After games on Fridays, Dad sometimes picked us up and we went to his house, which shared the alley with Atwater's Cafeteria."

Atwater's Cafeteria was an all-black-owned restaurant at the corner of 9th Street and 22nd Avenue South where my grandfather owned several properties.

He said he personally didn't eat there a lot but his father definitely was there all the time having breakfast. I find myself smiling again because I remember the way my grandfather used to like his eggs, which were sunny side up. As a kid, I wasn't with it, but I like the story he used to tell me about why they call the egg sunny-side up. "Not cooking the yolk of the egg reminds you of the rising sun," he said. Sometimes, depending on what Atwater's had on the menu, they would ask if he could smoke some meat on the smoker that was kept in the yard.

Feeling empowered, enlightened, and connected, I felt that this was a good place to end my questionnaire. I summarized to my uncle again the reasons for me wanting to write this book, so we can have all of our information in one spot. This can help us know more about our family because I don't know a lot. I'm not sure why my history was not a big interest to me growing up. Now that it is, I am making it my business to have the information that I discover available for everyone else in the family. This book will be a family tree for us, a family timeline.

I asked myself a question since I was embarking on what some would say is a journey, but what I now call a rooted journey home: how is a person to know where they're going if they don't know where they come from? Your family history is important, it's your story that you play an important role in. Having knowledge of the roots of your family is much like a piece of wood being added to a dying fire. Knowing your history ensures your family story never burns out. We are more connected to our ancestors than we know, I am a living witness to that. This *conversation with my uncle confirmed that my desire for avocado and beets wasn't a coincidence. I love upside-down pineapple cake and that was my uncle's favorite thing my grandmother made. My grandmother enjoyed shaking a leg.*

All these things that resonated with me and showed up in my life were being channelled from my grandparents. I strongly believe that we are our ancestors' dreams in the flesh. That there is some of whom your ancestors were in all of us. What would you say I was experiencing? Or do you think this is just a coincidence?

As this topic faded and came to an end, we found our way to the memory about a dog he used to have. This was one that I remembered very well because I feared him. He was this big lion-looking dog. Rosco, I believe his name was. he wasn't the color of a lion but he was built like one. He also had that thick, circular, spiky hair thing going on. I got over my fear, lol I chuckled out loud on that…I know now as an adult that all that you fear, to some degree, you'll have to face. And some of those sap suckers you'll have to face head-on!

He shared how he doesn't do too much nowadays. Said he was slowly working on the car. We spoke about him taking the gas tank out of his truck and some of the things he's currently doing around the house. "Nothing major," he ended with.

Chapter 3

THE VAIL IS TOREN

So I just arrived at Auntie Wanda's house, excited, especially after the in-depth conversation I had with my uncle. Wanda K. Burgess was the second-born child and first girl of my grandfather. I was waiting on her to put some clothes on because I told her that we were getting out of the house, not staying in. It was a beautiful day outside. I began questioning her about these Amazon packages on her doorstep. She said those were not her packages, they belonged to my little cousin Sanitra. Wanda raised her, but she's my Auntie

Chantay's daughter. So much of her story reminded me of my own. Being raised by a sister of your mother is one of the many things we had in common. Chantay was the youngest of my grandmother and grandfather's children.

We lost her about seven years ago. I was starting to get in my feelings after remembering this fact, so I changed the subject. I started to go ahead and ask Auntie Wanda questions while she was in the process of getting dressed. That was the least I could do, seeing as I did just pop up without any warning.

She does not do many recreational things. Come to think of it, she never really has. She was the homebody out of my grandfather's children. She would get out and do things on the weekend every now and then, but never during the week. Not much had changed from when I was a child until now. When I was younger, she worked at Campbell Park Elementary School in the kitchen, so she was up and out before dawn. If she went anywhere, it was up to Blackies to have a few beers with the guys. Blackies is still in business at the same location, run by the same black family. I typed that with such excitement for several reasons along with several feelings behind the thought.

Let Us Go Back, Back in Time

St. Petersburg's at one point had many stores and storefronts like Blackies, run and owned by people who look like me. 22nd Street was once the heart of the city, according to authors Rosalie Peck and Jon Wilson. 22nd Street, when described to me, sounded like something really far-fetched. This scenario isn't something that would even be seen in a movie at this time. Very few existed that highlighted the black excellence movement Mr. James (a co-worker) spoke about. It wasn't in my era, you could not find it in my history books unless you consider the one-sided story that was told to us about history. That glorified the hunt that everyone who looked like me was only slaves and part of towns and cities because we were dropped off there by way of boat.

Now don't shoot the messenger, she's only a little girl who believed what was taught to her. Especially from the school system, which, in my opinion, is one of the largest forms of propaganda. I was only given controlled information, which programmed me into seeing their perspective. Don't shoot the little girl, who now as an adult, understands self-hate was a side effect of the programming. She believed that people with the same color skin as her were only good at being slaves. That black people are what they called us, and that is one of the better terms. They said we could not think and were not intelligent or smart. But they could not read or write because that education was kept away from them since they weren't even considered human.

I repeat that 22nd Street, also known as the Ducasse that Mr. James told me about with a sense of pride and a gleam of light in his eyes, was known for being the heartbeat of the city. Nearby was a local projects called James Town, where the famous actress Angela Bassett once lived. Where later down the line they would turn the community event space that was being used for all sorts of things, church, weddings, parties and more, into the Dr. Carter G Woodson African American Museum.

Known as the father of African American history, he had a dual purpose of giving black Americans a history to be proud of and to ensure that the overlooked role of black people in American history was acknowledged by white historians. I want to be a part of the magic Dr. Carter G. Woodson foresaw. Something that's bigger than me. I now realize as an adult that I can see both sides of the coin, I'm our history, my history, and the hi(STORY) that will tell the story of just how extubating it is to be (copper-coloured) black. There is nothing generationally cursed about us as a people, we were (emphasis on were) just unlearned, and misguided.

Mr. James said The Ducasse had everything you wanted and needed. It had ice cream at Sno-Peak shops, jukeboxes and more. There was no-nonsense, just simple, fun times.

As a treat, a gift to myself, I bought *St. Petersburg's Historic 22nd Street South* by Rosalie Peck and Jon Wilson to help me learn more about the place I grew up in.

The book has pictures that give you a visual, yet they didn't slack in the written details that gave this black and white book so much color. Salons, drug stores, produces, clothing stores, Mercy Hospital, Manhattan Casino, The Royal Theater, Johnny Swain the butcher, S&S grocery that would wrap meat for wardrobes or home décor when people were hard up, bars, and more. There was no need to go anywhere else, but if that was not enough, the Ducasse also had a section that the teenagers could call home.

Words do give life, and they also add color. I have a motto: renewing your mindset changes the narrative, changing your thoughts, creating the picture, and transforming your words adds the color.

In my personal opinion, the whole book shouldn't talk about the contributions African Americans play in the invention of many things. Information like this should go into books marked history, better yet, Black History. How do the children given the title, Negro, Black, or African American, know where we are going if we don't know where we come from and are not being given the facts or accurate information from history?

That brings us back to the now, the present. It's a good place to segue back to the reason I was visiting Auntie Wanda. As she got ready, I filled her in on the reason for my unexpected visit. Trying to answer the question of, how do we know where we are going if we don't know where we come from? The heavy thought that has been banging from inside of me, from one of these new places I discovered has now become a hard pill I was trying to swallow. After I told myself I was no longer just going to be doing it for the vine (lol) or anyone else for that matter. I was no longer just showing up and putting my energy toward people, places, things, and thoughts that serve no purpose.

So, here I am at the oldest of my grandparent's children's house with so many questions. There's a part in *Finding Sierra*, my first book, where I say I am up, I am up, no more being Sleeping Beauty. It was time to ask more questions, time to change the narrative. It was time I throw myself in the fire!

> Life shrinks or expands in proportion to one's heART language

DEACON CLARK

Chapter 4

INQUIRING HEARTS WANT TO KNOW

There is no wonder how I ended up in this head and heart space, feeling like I have been sleeping and just waking up. Where am I, who am I, and how did I get here?

Sierra - "I am here, Auntie, because I decided to write a second book and I want it to be about my grandfather. The seed that started my branch on this family tree. The man behind it all. I want to know about your father…my grandfather is a mystery to me."

To my surprise, she threw it back at me and said through the bathroom door: "Momma is also a mystery woman because we know truly little of who she is."

My aunt is in the same unlearned place as I am. How could this be, how could she not know intimate details about the woman who birthed her? This was not good and very alarming, panic kicked in, but I didn't show it. My heart was saddening for me and her. I could now feel the wavering (spirit) emotions.

I just assumed with her being the oldest of my grandparents' children, the first child born, she would have all the juicy details to fill in my blanks but she knows truly little. This is now a state of emergency in my world. Who are these mysterious grandparents of mine? I have to be honest, a part of me was very intrigued by the lack of information, the *Indiana Jones, Monk, House, Cold Case, C.S.I Miami* detective part of me felt like we just got the case of our life. A case that I was the lead detective on, a case that would change my whole career when I solved it.

Wanda - "I have no recollection of who my mother's father was or much about my mother's upbringing. What school she went to, if she had sisters and brothers, what was her father's name was, and things like that."

Now, my *Indiana Jones, Inspector Gadget* and *C.S.I* mode has kicked in for real, for real.

I have a real-life mystery that I am about to uncover. She went on to say that she talked to her daughter, Erica, who is her only child, and Sanitra about doing an ancestral DNA so we can find out more information. I thought it was a good idea, although a part of me is slightly skeptical about that process, but at this point, if it could give me any kind of information on where my grandmother and parents came from, that could help solve the mystery. I know that my grandfather came from Belize, and I thought my grandmother came from Lake City, but where are her roots from? Where are her mother and father from? I understand Auntie Wanda's concern and the idea of wanting to do an ancestral DNA test so we can find out this information. She was perplexed at not knowing, her exact words were, "Point blank straight up, even being the oldest I don't know that much about my mother or my grandmother."

Although this lady was her mother, she knew very little of who she was outside of that fact. Her mother's mother's name was Catherine and from the conversation with my uncle, he said her last name was Hancock or Hangcock. I mentioned that to Auntie Wanda but she was not 100% sure about that information herself. I know panic sounded like a premature word to use earlier but can you empathize with me now? You see why research and talking to everyone is going to be critical because although they are the children of my grandparents, they were born at different times, they all have different perspectives and they all see from different views.

I get to put this together like a puzzle and create a picture of my family tree, my family's history. It seems we know more about my grandfather's side than we know of my grandmother's bloodline. From what I do know, co-signed by Desmond and Wanda, is that Grandma was from Lake City. His kids knowing more about him than their mother is so ironic since he was an immigrant and knowing less about your father's side was common in my era. This did make me smile to know that my grandfather was a good father and then some!

I have a confession to make that maybe three years ago, I was nudged by something to reach out to my grandfather's last living sibling, Lucille. It breaks my heart to say that I never went to the nursing home to visit her. There's life, then there's the compass of your soul, which I didn't understand at that moment. I was trying to tell myself why that visit could have been so profound. If I had listened to my natural GPS when it wanted to lead me there, imagine the things I could have learned about my grandfather that only his sister could have told me. Going to my grandfather's siblings' children was now my only way of finding answers, the only way I was going to put this puzzle together. Kenny, who my uncle Desmond referenced when I visited him, is Lucille's son.

Ok, let me catch you up. Really, I'm catching myself up also. So, Kenny, Desmond, and Sylvia are all first cousins, which means their parents were siblings.

Sierra - "Who was Sylvia to Marjorie?"

Wanda - "Aunt Marjorie was Sylvia's mother."

Marjorie, Pearly, and Lucille are the names of my grandfather's sisters. Sylvia is my grandfather's oldest niece.

Okay, jumping back on the topic of the ancestry DNA. It seems like a brilliant idea now. Doing one with the oldest of my grandfather's children and the oldest of his sibling's children, which would be Sylvia. I will investigate it and see how much it costs.

Wanda - "I really don't know that much about mama. As a little girl, I remember living in Lake City Florida. I remember that we lived between a railroad track, which back in the days they called one side of the railroad the Nigger section and the other side the white section. And all I remember is that Mama told me that she was with Larry… daddy…and that they found him on a railroad track in Lake City."

Sierra, in a high-pitched voice from excitement, because the only thing I remember hearing is found on railroad tracks and right before that, Larry! I cut her off by shouting out - "LARRY WAS FOUND ON THE RAILROAD TRACKS."

Wanda - "No! No! No!" Stopping mid-sentence to reply to my outburst…"Daddy was found."

Sierra - "Grandaddy."

Wanda - "Yes! Daddy, my daddy, your grandaddy (me) really! Your granddaddy."

Sierra - "On a railroad track!"

Sierra - "Really, Auntie!" I said in a high-pitched voice. She did a belly jiggle kind of laugh, much like Desmond when he recalled a few memories.

Wanda - "It was him and his friends in a service uniform. I don't know what ship was docked in that zone at the time. I don't know if it was Jacksonville, Florida, or somewhere else in Florida where he and his friends got together and came to this town and got drunk. The story says he never made it back to the ship. I don't know if his friends left him, or he got with a girl, and he was on the railroad tracks drunk."

She saw my mouth still open and added bass to her voice as she slowly continued.

"Larry, daddy, my momma, which is your grandma, found your grandaddy on the railroad track. I don't know what happened. He got so drunk he didn't know where he was. My mama brought him back to the house somehow. I don't know if he made his way back to the ship, stayed there, or they stayed connected. Either way, Daddy and Momma got together at some point, and that is where I came in at. (She was back to talking in her regular voice). But I was left in Lake City, with Grandma, her momma."

Sierra - "Katherine…"

Wanda - "Yea, with a C."

Sierra - "Oh, a C…I spelled it with a K."

Wanda started stuttering as if she was about to make a confession. "I don't know her last name," she said, sounding like it was painful yet it provided a degree of relief also.

Sierra - "No middle name?"

Wanda - "I don't even know that! I don't know if she was married or had a boyfriend. There was a man that was always there."

Sierra - "That is that friend."

Wanda - "That was not Mr. Willie, though."

Sierra - "Oh ok, but I have no clue who Mr. Willie was. Who's Mr. Willie?"

Wanda - "Mr. Willie came along after they moved from Lake City. They ran into each other at a bar somewhere."

I was still very lost on who Mr. Willie was, so I asked another question to see if I could figure this out. "So, Grandma ran into Mr. Willie even after you were born?"

Wanda replied yes with excitement. Like she was happy that I figured it out. I was still very much confused, more now than before. Why did she sound like she was happy about that? I had to laugh at myself, it was my turn to do the belly jiggle laugh. It wasn't until I was typing this and listening to the recording from the interview that I realized why I was so confused as to who Mr. Willie was.

When Wanda said grandma, I thought she was talking about my grandmother, her mother, not her grandma (Katherine, still unsure with a K or C) her mother's mother. So, when she said he met grandmother, she meant her grandmother met a Mr. Willie. Belly jiggling funny. The color brought clarity to this picture. My grandparents moved my great-grandmother from Lake City to St. Petersburg, Florida.

Auntie Wanda says she remembers the car ride. This place she remembers as the new location was called Royal Courts. I clearly remember Uncle Desmond mentioning that Royal Courts was the place they lived before moving to Union Street, which I still consider my grandma's house to this day. I'm not 100% sure whose new location it is. Is it the address of the Burgess residence? Or the place my great-gramma was going to call home?

Sierra, in my high-pitched voice - "Is Royal Courts over by the hump off 4th Street?"

Wanda - "No."

Sierra - "No?"

Wanda - "No, Royal Courts was on 16th Street."

Sierra - "16th Street?"

Wanda - "Yeah, and 3rd Avenue. That is where the dome sits at. It's still where it currently sits."

This Royal Courts area she speaks of was the beginning of modern-day genocide, not a physical genocide like the Black Wall Street massacre in 1921. But, where the death of family, community, hopes, and dreams died instead. Travelers Rest Church was a big white church on that sidewall on 22nd Avenue and 16th Street.

I just so happened to look up while she was talking and noticed a gray streak going down the middle of her head. I told her it was becoming of her. I just saw on my Facebook memory an old picture of my mama and me and she had it too, in the same place. Right at the front, the middle part of their head. She said it had been standing out lately.

We went on to agree on how much her hair is like her father's. Nice texture and salt and pepper. I loved my grandfather's hair. It was not until after I interlocked my hair that I noticed it was the same texture. As a child, my hair was permed so it never had the chance to reveal its natural texture. Although I had been natural for a while before embarking on my sister loc journey, I still never saw my hair's full potential. It would draw up so bad, making it very thick and hard to comb.

I would get so aggravated that if I owned a pair of clippers at those moments, I would have cut it off. I knew that I no longer wanted to feel hostage by the hair industry any longer. It's a bonus when you eliminate any kind of chemicals on you or in you. So, staying natural was necessary, but I needed to find a less stressful way of doing that. I did my research between dreads and sister locs, and I chose sister locs. I am so glad I did. Many said that I was not going to last a year and my ex-husband I was with at the time was against natural hair. Still, I allowed none of that to change my decision.

INQUIRING HEARTS WANT TO KNOW

Five years later, it's a lifestyle, no longer a journey. I had no idea that going back to my natural hair was going to come with so many benefits. I touch my hair more, I look at my hair more and I like looking at myself. I could always SEE that I looked beautiful, now I FEEL beautiful, inside and out. There's a difference. Now they have so many products to support your natural hair journey. Being natural is back, and there's even a saying, "Don't let the shrinkage fool you!"

Chapter 5

GENERATIONALLY CURSED OR JUST UNLEARNED

Auntie Wanda jumped back to the discussion by saying she wanted to do the DNA thing; she really wanted to have this process done. Still, trying to get her out of the house I said, "OK, let's rock and roll," as I interrupted her to ask if she had her shoes on. I was ready to feel the sun on my skin. Not to mention that my stomach was starting to speak up as well. She replied, "No," as she started walking toward her bedroom. I assured her we could drive and talk, although she continued with what she was saying. "I want to know about my grandmother," she said. I knew where she was coming from. I felt her desire to want to know.

Hence the reason for my visit was to pick her brain about my grandfather. You hear a lot about families being cursed. It now hit me that families are not cursed. We are just passing down the same unlearned behaviors. We will overcome this by having family discussions without judgement. Creating family goals and having daily interaction. It's ok to disagree but do it in an intentional space filled with structure and love. This will eliminate the damage we are causing and passing down and create clarity so healthy decisions are made. Also if we stand on the backs of our scared ancestors, we can learn from the ways of old. Knowing better mandates you to do better. Living and learning will change our narrative and disrupt the old traumatic ways of doing not just family, but all things. I know better, so I am definitely going to do better by being that change I want to see.

Wanda - "I want to know where my mother came from. I want to know where my grandmother came from. We have no documentation on my grandmother's history or my father's history, we only know where he was born. We know his siblings but as far as my bloodline or who my mother really is, we know nothing. The little I do know is that my mother said her mother Catherine came from Carolina, but what part of Carolina? I am uncertain."

I inquired about my grandfather's last name at that moment because my grandmother has Burgess from marrying my granddad, or did that name come from Larry's father, the gentleman that she was with prior? Because after speaking to my uncle, he was going back and forth on whether my grandparents were even married or if they were still married at the time that I was born. She said Burgess had come from my grandfather. Another reason I wanted to know was because when I was talking to Scrap Patty's son August, he asked if Burgess was our grandfather's last name because if you came from Belize, he felt like Burgess was way too Americanized to be his last name.

She said that was the name that we know of and that was the name that was documented. I wondered then if he spoke a different language, so I asked. She said he spoke Spanish and he also spoke French. She did give me a little history lesson on how the majority of Britain spoke French rather than Spanish before they were taken over and remained Great Britain from the British. She also said you had the low-life Italians and the low-life Germans that were there and when Britain took over, they put them all on boats and brought them to America.

Auntie Wanda went into the bathroom to use it before we left the house. I took this moment to just recollect some of the things that I just learned. My grandfather was found on the railroad track, and so many things were happening to me at that moment. This is so super cool, I never would have guessed that I would be learning this information when I decided to draft this book.

I thought I was going to find out about a hard-working man, my grandfather. This book took a turn, a very unexpected, yet delightful one. So much for the base of this book being about my grandfather, I guess you can say it still is. Everything started with him, so he is the truth, he planted the seed, and he is my rooted way home. But we know that it's a woman that gives life, so my grandmother is as important as my grandfather.

I began to question myself about what took me so long to even ask these questions. What took so long, why have I never inquired about this information before? This is what I meant by my earlier statement: we are not learned, we passed down unlearned behavior. We passed down certain things to our next generation and as you see, my aunt herself didn't inquire about her grandmother, her mother's mother, or her father's mother.

I didn't either, so if that isn't learned behavior right in front of your face, I don't know what is. From what I know so far, we are not cursed as a family but I see signs in areas that show we were unlearned at one point in time. Why have I not known these things? I feel like, oh my goodness, this excites me. It really excites me. Not only am I learning where I come from, but again, how can I know where I'm going if I don't know where I come from? Some people might beg to differ but those who feel what I'm saying understand what I'm saying.

I now finally have my keys in hand, a fine time to ask Auntie Wanda where she wants to go eat. "What do you have a taste for Auntie? Is there anywhere you've been wanting to go but haven't been?"

Completely ignoring me, she said, "What was the weather like outside?"

Sierra - "You'll find out once we get out there," I said in my can we go already voice.

One hand on the doorknob, keys in the other, she walks toward me and confesses that she's not wearing a bra, which is nothing new because all my life I have known her to not be a big bra fan. She wore them to work and appointments only. Is this why I am not fond of them myself? Could there be some truth behind why I don't like wearing bras? I cannot even tell you what my bra size is, I hardly ever wear one, but since she brought up not wearing a bra, let us explore my perspective or some thoughts around this. I didn't even notice she didn't have one on. Want to talk about it? Here we go! So I tell her, of course I know, her nipples were featured in my first book as well. Since I can remember Auntie Wanda never wore a bra, she stayed in a white T-shirt, nipple poking out like you had tied the end of a balloon.

I have always felt that it brought way too much attention but she never really cared. And because I didn't like wearing bras either, I would just push my nipples in to avoid extra attention. So, I adapted to pushing my nipples in as a young girl. I didn't want nipples like Auntie Wanda. I intentionally pushed them in so much that I remember going for a check-up in high school when I was getting my annual exam. The doctor said to me that I shouldn't do that. He was startled that one of my nipples looked like an inward belly button. The look on his face said he was genuinely concerned. He had to inquire, I think his mind wouldn't allow him not to. I told him how they got that way, the same story I just told you. His medical advice to me was to no longer do that because my nipples could grow inward and that would be painful and cause other problems.

But going braless must be a thing now as I see so many women doing it. I love it. Long story short, Auntie Wanda is 71 and still doesn't like wearing bras. I confirmed her age as we walked to the car, and I let her know that I was putting this in the book because she mentioned the topic.

We finally made it in the car 45 minutes later, and ancestry DNA was still the topic at hand, which lets me know that she is in the same place I am, wanting to know about our history. She said again, "I just want to know who my mother is and who my grandmother was." Since interviewing my aunt, I made sure to tell everyone to talk with the elders in the family. Get the (game) untold stories, before it's lost forever. Knowing a family trait can be very vital information to some medically. Wanda started describing her grandmother's features.

It got a little confusing (again) for a moment because she was saying grandma and I was saying grandma, but she was referring to her mother's mother and I was referring to my mother's mother. Once I got it together, I realized she was talking about my great-grandmother who had hips like Patti, a butt like Auntie Chantay, and pecan skin color. She was now talking about her father and his features, and how he was always in shape. She smiled when bragging about her father being an amazing swimmer. She could remember always being by the water with him as he intentionally made sure they went by the water as a family.

She spoke of how my grandfather would wreck my grandmother's nerves because he would get out in the water and swim far, far, far, far out way past the buoys. Momma was always concerned that something was going to eat him out there. He could swim like a fish, so she called him Hercules. Daddy was built too, he had good bones.

"I got good bones," I say and smile. It's a country song that says something about having good bones. Her comment made me think about how when my little cousins were younger, you could see a muscular physique. I pointed out Tony and Linwood in particular, and so I was a little baffled at this moment because she was telling me how strong my grandfather looked. I have seen a picture of him with a muscular physique. In one of the pictures I remember, he was picking this man up. He was wrapped around his bicep and holding him in the air with one arm.

I also remember us dropping him off at dialysis, unaware of what dialysis was at that time. I just know he had to go twice a week. Depending on how bad your condition is, when your liver no longer functions at the normal capacity it was designed for, you have to go to dialysis. I couldn't understand how this Hercules man that she just described to me was on dialysis.

Now I had all kinds of questions, so I asked how long he was on dialysis.

Wanda - "One day, he just got sick, and he went to Bayfront. Then suddenly, they said he had kidney failure."

She said then she knew he had to go on the machine for dialysis. She started describing what that meant for him. He had to go be connected to a machine and filter his blood out. She said it didn't do him any good, he only got sicker and sicker. Then they talked about his life being shortened if he didn't get a new kidney. I wondered if he was on the kidney transplant list. Wait, did they have a kidney transplant list back then? I wondered…

Wanda - "Kidney transplant list?" She chuckled at that moment with as much sarcasm as she could find and said, "Why on Earth would they want to put a black man on the kidney transplant list?"

I know so much more now than I did then. She mentioned him needing to have these ports connected to him, which I am a little familiar with because I had a friend who was on dialysis, so I got an up-close and personal experience from that, but my grandfather had more than one port on him.

When she started describing the plastic things in his arms, I had a flashback. It was so clear. I could see them being in both arms. Now that I have been in the medical field for a few years, I have more experience and understanding. Honestly, I wished I didn't, especially after her next statement. She said not only were they in both of his arms, but he also had one in his upper thigh.

She reported they were in at least four or five places. This just made me cringe and my eyes even watered a little because that's just how visual the picture that I saw was. I have now added color to the picture, making it more realistic.

Chapter 6

A DIVIDED HOUSE

I wanted to shake off that feeling, so I changed the subject. I asked her how old she was when Grandmother and Granddaddy separated.

Wanda - "Momma and Daddy got into a fight, he left, and this time didn't come back. He also had him a side girlfriend who had five children or something like that."

My brain is on go, being told these stories, and the pages are turning rapidly in my head. It's like what I mentioned earlier, how words give life. Feeling empowered, feeling like somebody, I know this is just the tip of the iceberg. Adding color to what once was black and white that I could hardly see until now. Interviewing everyone is bringing it to life. When I interviewed Eric Atwater, he mentioned this family and just like that, a piece to this puzzle could be applied.

I just talked to Sanitra four days before. She was trying to explain to me who George was. George was the lady's son who my grandfather was with. Sanitra kept saying, "You know him, you know him," and I kept saying I didn't. I do have vague memories of who he was. Although when having that discussion with her, it didn't click. Then when I was talking to Auntie Wanda, the color appeared.

I remember her, I remember her children being around. Granddad was going back and forth between her and this lady and taking her and her children places. My grandfather was a family-oriented person, so he loved the kids.

It was a predominantly white neighborhood. There were only two African American families on the block. When they moved to Union Street, the only black families were my grandmother and the people at the corner house, which shocked me, so I interrupted her.

Sierra - "I never seen anyone besides once or twice when a car parked there during my childhood at this house, never any children. I remember playing with children in each house on the street except for that one."

She assured me it was an African family that lived there and later, the Roachs moved into the neighborhood. Not roaches as in cockroaches, Roach was the last name of the family who moved in next door. She spoke briefly about the Catholic church that was across the street.

Wanda - "I would see from time to time, nuns come and go. They operated a preschool/daycare of some sorts."

I didn't say it aloud, because I had already interrupted her several times as she was talking, but I remember having thoughts as a teenager of wanting to become a nun.

A DIVIDED HOUSE

Wanda - "I was about 13 when we moved over to Union St. When Momma had to go to work, she would drop us off over to the house where daddy and Otha-lee were staying since they were now dating. She would come to pick us back up when she got off. When we were old enough to get jobs, we would help Momma pay the bills at the house."

Sierra - "Where was your first job?"

Wanda - "At Webb City."

Around the time she was getting ready to graduate she was working and going to school at Lakewood. My mom said she went to Bogey, so I was a little concerned about how Auntie Wanda went to Lakewood High School and her sisters went to another high school. Same household, different high school. They split up everybody and sent them to different schools. So, they bussed them all over she said.

She remembers going to Bogie for a little while, but she said she's not sure exactly why she ended up going to Lakewood. She said they talked about them since they came out of an all-black school, which was 16th Street Middle School at the time. Being mistreated because they came from the Southside. People said they weren't smart enough to be in an interracial school with white kids. Wanda is an open mic… she was popping off. From one topic to another, like she had been dying to have this conversation with someone. I'm so glad it was me that she was talking to.

She then started telling me how she recalls, when she was at 16th Street Middle School, there were people that would come in periodically, sit with them in a room and test them by showing them pictures of things.

I asked, "So, they were experimenting on y'all?" and she said absolutely, and this went on for a few weeks. They would call children out of the classrooms one by one, take them inside of a room, sit them in a chair, and ask them all kinds of questions. Showing them pictures to see if they were smart enough or whatever they were looking for. Was this being done at all-white schools? Did my grandmother know about this? Was this to rule out who was fit, smart, or dumb to decide if it was okay to go to the white schools?

At this time, you had elementary, middle school, and high school all in one school. There was no separation, so you had the adult kids going to school with the little kids. She was trying to explain to me how you had babies going to school with teenage boys who have hormones, and they were around the little girls and the little boys. She felt that was not right. She expressed that the little children were being influenced, touched, and raped by their upper classmates. Now I don't know if this was a concern or a real thing that was happening.

Could this be the reason why schools are now separated? She said her mother was smart, although not book smart, and she told them to speak up for themselves. When they would say that they were not up to par and could not read.

Wanda - "They had us reading at a certain grade level if you want to say that. They had us reading the same exact thing over and over each year."

Sierra - "Reading what?"

Wanda - "For example, Sally, Dick and Jane knew how to run. Sally, Dick and Jane jumped over the wall. I remember doing this for at least four years straight. Momma would say how are you not educated when it's their curriculum that they are giving you to learn?"

Sierra - "WOW, drop the mic Elnora (grandma). They still call our children uneducated but they're learning what was being provided for them to learn."

Wanda - "Remember me challenging the school system?"

When my cousin Sanitra was going to school, she would go back and forth with the school board because they wanted to say Sanitra wasn't smart and couldn't read. They wanted to put her in special classes, and she said no. If she was learning the material that y'all were giving her, how can she not read? So, she challenged them every time and didn't allow them to put her in the special class. What she wanted to point out is still going on now to this day, they are teaching the same curriculum to our children. Yes, a few things have been adjusted, writing in cursive has been taken away, but the overall school system is a joke. They are still classifying our children as being illiterate, not smart enough, and not being able to comprehend information.

Chapter 7

NO, YOU MAY NOT

I can tell my aunt has been waiting and wanting to have some of these conversations.

Wanda - "Momma would have us doing certain things around the house. We would cut the grass and the hedges, trim the bushes, and clean the house. We could comprehend information very well."

As she was speaking, a visual came to me. I remember my grandma having the world encyclopedias on the shelves, and the National Geographic out on the table for us to see.

Wanda - "Momma's way of educating us was more effective than what we learned after sitting in schoolhouses for five days. Twelve years of programming. Being programmed how to think the way they would want us to think. And then even after we do that, they still classify us as being dumb and illiterate."

They are still sending our children to schoolhouses five days a week. A new survey says the average American uses just 37% of the information they learn in school. Do you believe that after all this time, they are saying we are still dumb? How is it that from that generation to my generation this is still a thing? The survey of 2,000 adults commissioned by H&R Block found that 84% of the people learning things in school said that they have never used that knowledge after graduation. The average respondent also said that over half of the skills they use in the workforce were learned on the job, rather than in school.

Let's make the school system great, being that most parents have to work. So, someone must see after the children. Our babies are with their teachers more than they are with their parents but many will say that raising a child starts at home.

Now I was on that gravy boat when it was selling at one point. Auntie Wanda added color to that thought and the place where that puzzle went. It just breaks my heart. It is hard to do when parents are absent from homes, having to maintain two or three jobs just to make ends meet. That is getting by, which means there is a lack of money because to have anything, you need money. Everything costs SOMETHING and I am not against things costing money when emergencies happen in life unexpectedly. Collecting rainwater and growing crops without paying fines and fees. People are paying for air space now, did you know that? Using the same graph as the one that divided land up.

NO, YOU MAY NOT

Their regulations and approval are needed to do things on a free planet that we all reside on. Where it is a gift to everybody. That is just my two cents on it. For those placed in charge to ensure the liberty bell rings, justice for all being for a select few plays a big part in the propaganda and unlearned behavior displayed.

I get it, we all cannot run the planet, somebody needs to be in charge. They spend all year teaching us, and at the end, they still classify us as dumb and illiterate or not being able to comprehend. Then why keep doing what is not working? Hell, this sounds and feels like unlearned behavior to me.

The school system is still teaching the same curriculum to the next generation and then it hit me, if you have classified this as education to prepare them for the real world then why are they still being classified as illiterate and dumb when they come out of your system? The government is fine with you being dumb, stupid, and crazy. They will keep you in the lowest form they can. My aunt said this is their way of keeping people that look like us suppressed.

I must admit, as a child, me, and my cousin said Wanda was crazy when she used to tell us different things. Her sisters still say it. But she wanted us to step outside the box that they were trying to put us in, deprogramming our minds.

22nd St S, 5th Ave, and 18th Ave, all these spots used to be swinging with black people and black businesses. She started talking about the dome and all the families that lost their homes due to the city leaders' plans to build the dome to lure the Major League Baseball Team in the 1980s. The grand opening day of the new Florida Suncoast Dome was celebrated on Feb 28, 1990. It's sad that I'm just learning these things. The location of the dome was where black families once lived and from which they were displaced. More than 2,000 hearts, because home is where the heart is, were uprooted, along with their places of worship and businesses.

How and why am I just desiring to devour this information? This is one of the reasons I decided to write this book. This is not about the black and white thing; I repeat this is not about a race thing. Although people not liking you because of the color of your skin is a real thing.

Yet it's not the focus. I was just watching a video of a native of St. Pete sharing her experience when Project Sun Dome was in full effect. She said her house, her grandmother's house, used to sit where the Dome currently sits. A lot of resemblance in Aunt Wanda's story. In the interview, she said they came in promising money and jobs to the people who gave up their homes so they could put a stadium there for a team that they didn't even have yet.

Then she said how it was heartbreaking because when talking to her children, she wanted to tell them about the house she grew up in and the church that they were baptized in. All gone! Therefore, I called it genocide of family, community, hopes, and dreams. And just like that, all those landmarks no longer existed anymore. I can only imagine how that made her feel. This story is one of the reasons behind my wanting to write this book. It reminds me of having to see the house I spent a lot of my childhood in with my granddad. For that to not be a part of my adult story, it does feel like being robbed of something.

I don't know what would be worse, no longer being able to see the landmark like the lady described in the video. Or still being able to see the landmark and know that it is occupied by another family. This is why I am doing all that I can to make sure that we save this property, the one my uncle mentioned when I interviewed him. I have had to separate family from legacy so I can stay out of my feelings. Not everyone in the family sees the bigger picture. I was wasting energy trying to get them to see it. That is not my job, but it is my opportunity to honor my grandfather.

I have every intention of doing so. This is the last one that we have, now that I am old enough, not a little girl, but of an age to do something about it. I don't want to ride past there like I have to ride past the other house and see somebody else occupying it. Not by the hair of my chinny chin chin. And thanks to Elnora, I have hair on my chin lol…

Chapter 8

FAMILY LEGACY

Creating a family bank account can benefit my family as it can help my little cousin pay cash for school, buy cars, etc. We can start a family business and keep things in the family. That way, if school systems don't improve, they don't have to go to their schools and learn their curriculum and be programmed. My family won't have to go into debt for anything. Especially when it's time to bury a loved one as we experienced with the last two deaths in my family.

Doesn't a family business have a good ring to it, being financially free? Living with options is what money allows. Establishing our own family system, that way, my little boy cousins won't have to worry about applying for a job. A few of them have already been in trouble with the law, so right now, they would have to jump through hoops to get a job.

Even after time served, no matter how long that record was done away with, that's all they see. Just today, my little cousin shared a post on Facebook that said, "Why can't felons who changed their LIFESTYLE be accepted? America accepts everything else. You are never forgiven you are never good enough, even after you paid your time and fines, and attended the classes you needed. Yet still, they throw those things in your face. Even if you are out here trying to do right, live in their system and by their rules."

Society wants us to get a nine to five and send our children to college, then they are in debt before they are even 21. It costs thousands of dollars to go to college, with those interest fees. Family wealth or having a family business can eliminate that. They can work at a family-owned business and not accumulate debt.

I was driving in circles as we talked, I wanted to go to Big Storm Brewery on 66th St N so I could have her try some craft beer. We ended up at Madeira Beach. Colt 45 used to be her beer back in the day. I can still picture what the can looked like, even today. She always bought cans, never bottles. They were silver with black specks all over and a blue bull with that ring in his nose.

Despite the setting, I must admit that my spirit was a little disturbed at the treatment of a certain class of people and how this is still going on. They have just found diverse ways of doing it.

FAMILY LEGACY

It's Personal, Part II

Wanda - "What's new in your life? I don't think we had a nice talk since your 40th birthday party."

I was newly divorced, in denial about having to file for bankruptcy, and didn't want to accept my new normal. I was hiding from all my potential. We had a moment, even at my birthday party, when she finally saw that I was not a little girl anymore. I was an adult now. I say that because as a parent, we always see our children as our babies. I titled my 40th party I'm coming out, Using Diana Ross' *I'm coming out* as the theme song. This is exactly what I was doing. I wanted to make sure that everybody knew that because I was tired of my own crap but also tired of people not taking me seriously.

Wanda and I had a little spit during my birthday party. It was no hard feelings, it was all out of love. It had to be done. She was able to see that Sierra was no longer a shy, timid young lady. It was even said to me by several people during that time..."You think you're grown now?" Some even asked me, "Who are you talking to?" referring to my tone. They said, "Oh you done learned how to talk junk, and now you want to talk junk to everybody." I even had to set the record straight for a few people. I was not talking junk, I was just actually finally speaking up! Saying how I felt. For a long time, I didn't say anything, for a long time, I didn't express how I felt.

If you were standing on my toe, I would never say ouch, I would never even inform you that you were standing on my toe. I never made a facial expression that showed any signs of grief or discomfort. That is the version of Sierra that people were used to. That is the version of myself that I thought I had to be to show people around me that I loved them, at the expense of myself. I didn't want to accept my new normal, so I was hiding from all my potential.

Now, I was coming out! Coming out of a divorce, I was coming out of my shell. I was coming out of my complacency, coming out of the fear of who I was outside and what people wanted me to be. I need that to be known. I needed that to be loud and clear. I wanted that to be heard from the mountain top. I was doing exactly what I said I wanted to do that year. I'm coming out was my theme song for like three weeks. I can still faintly hear the music playing in my head even though the only thing I knew at that moment was the chorus. Something about the song spoke to me even though I had no idea who sang the song at that time, so I had to search for it and look for it.

Once I found it, I played it with the lyrics and the words of the song spoke exactly what I was feeling and thinking. This is huge for me because I had no problem, I got extraordinary joy from being what I call the behind-the-scenes person. I love being behind the scenes helping someone accomplish and do something, find things out about themselves, and then watch them grow and blossom. Then leave and never say that I did for them. Now even this song that is playing from inside of me is telling me that I need to come out from behind the curtain. It was my time, it's my time to be on the front line.

I must admit it was like learning a whole new Sierra all over again. I had to acquire new ways of functioning. It was like I had to learn to walk, talk, and think all over again, from unfamiliar places within me. Adding color to a different version of myself. This reminded me so much of Frankenstein. To be comfortable from behind the curtain, outside of my boxes, and free of my limitations. A new Sierra had to come alive

Chapter 9

ANGELS UNAWARE

I remember one night, standing behind Atwaters with my cousin Kimmie. I'm not sure who arrived first, me or her. This spot, was clearly a comfort zone, a secure place for my family over the years. Many of us come back here from time to time. I think adding the color has just helped me to see why. This is the alley I mentioned earlier when referring to the Hugh Burgess Estate. This is the alley where I was barefoot and snotty-nosed as a kid when those magical moments were being created while vising my grandfather.

There we were, posted up, as we called it. Not sure what prompted this as my destination, yet here we were. I decided to tell her that me and my husband at the time were getting a divorce. I shared with her my concerns about dating again and trying to get to know somebody nowadays. How that was scary in the world that we live in. Getting to know somebody all over again and being back in the dating world could be brutal.

I didn't want anything to do with it I said and without a second thought, her advice to me was, "You better get out there like you never left!"

I can admit that I was in a place where I felt like I didn't know who I was or what I was made of. She said what she said and I chewed on that thought for quite some time before I was able to use that as nourishment for my body. I now could take that understanding and raise it to an overstanding, allowing me to see clearly from my inner-standing.

I am out here Black Gurl like I never left. I am out here being all I can be. I am out here being the change I want to see. I am out here not to judge anyone, but to share my experience, my journey, and my lessons. I am out here being my ancestor's dreams in the flesh. I am out here leaving a mark and making it legendary. I am out here doing it for our last name. I am out here to be my part in freedom ringing.

I am out here, my Blu3 Ang3l...using it, no longer applying it. You would be so proud of me. I'm blooming my ass off!

I will say it again, how long I've been asleep saddens me. I'm wiping tears while I type as it sparks thoughts. Is this concept of being generationally cursed just that, being or staying asleep? Not seeing the truth behind something. Is being generationally cursed a CHOICE and not actually a curse at all? When we don't know any better, we cannot pass down any better knowledge. How do we expect our children to have a (promising) future with the same unlearned, self-stifling, victim mindset?

I'm still out here

Sierra, ready to change the subject - "Tell me about Uncle Larry."

Wanda - "Larry was a ladies' man. He had girlfriends all over."

Miss Juanita, who ended up being my auntie, put his player card away. He decided to marry her. He was extremely good at playing pool. Bare's Pool Room was like his second home, she said. They were younger but liked to hang out with their older brother when he went out at night.

Sierra - "So he and Uncle Desmand knew how to play pool?" Of course, I Interrupted her, with my excitement.

Wanda (who never stopped talking) - "Momma taught them that when they go out, they stay together, which is why I was so strict on you all about coming in the house and not having the same crew you left out the house with."

I had a real flashback that made me rub the back of my head because if we happened to come home in a different order than we left, she was there at the door waiting to pop us in the back of the head as we walked in.

I took this into my adult life when going out to the clubs with my girlfriends. If you came with me, you leave with me, I don't care how fine he was. If you decided you want to meet up with that gentleman later, then do that on your time, but I'm taking you back to where I picked you up from. My grandmother was trying to teach us valuable skills.

Perhaps that pop on the back of the head awakened something. I remember the time I had to pick my own switch from the tree. There were some hedges in between my grandmother's house and her best friend's house who lived to the left of us if you were coming down the street. Miss Willie B was her name and there were these bushes that often got these yellow, orange, and red berries on them. I remember eating them when we were younger. That was the same tree that we were told to go outside and get a switch from when it was time to get a spanking.

Switching the subject again because my thoughts were all over the place. I didn't want to stop asking questions that I felt were overdue. So, if I thought it, I asked it.

Sierra - "Did my mom never have a car?" I remember her driving at least once when I was having a party. It was my 21st birthday, I think. She was there at the party because she's my number one supporter. She had to drive my car home because I was in no condition to drive. None of my friends wanted to leave the party.

We had the party on 18th Avenue and 49th Street right there in that little plaza. All she had to do was drive straight down 18th Avenue, make two or three turns and she was home. I was so nervous, but I was not in a condition to do anything about it, so I told her to make sure she called me when she got home like I was the mother.

Wanda - "So what's your first book about?"

Sierra - "The book is about going from struggle to opportunity. Discovering the covert operation to the M.U.S. (made-up stuff) I believed from the things that occurred in my upbringing. I felt that I was missing out on something due to my parents not being present in my everyday life. I made up these stories that made me feel bad about myself. The thought and the underlying concept of what a good home should consist of wasn't my reality. It had me feeling like if you didn't grow up with a mother and a father inside the household then automatically, there was something wrong with you."

I took that along with me throughout my life. The only truth about that is the thought process that I put into it because I now know children who grew up with mothers and fathers in the household and they still got in trouble and rebelled. What's perfect? Save yourself, understand that words and people can only give you what they have to give.

They cannot give you any more or any less is what I realized. As a child, I had nothing to do with one or the other, it totally boils down to who you are as a person and what you are made of. She said she even knew when my grandparents did separate, they still visited each parent equally. They spent as much time with my grandad as they did with my grandmother. Despite how things went with them in their life, they were able to see both parents.

Sierra - "So, let me tell you while asking you. Did you know, that I was about nine years old when my grandmother told me that my mother was not my mother? It was Grandma who told me that Auntie Patti was not my mama. I thought Auntie Patti was my mother, I had no idea that she wasn't."

I mentioned in the first book that Grandma would call us into the room at separate times and give us a little snack. On this day, she told me that Patti was not my momma. That Duke was my mother, the only thing I knew about Duke at this moment was that she was the crackhead of the family. Then, I grew up and found out that Auntie Chantay was a crackhead as well. Although I'm not sure why but Chantay wasn't talked down about because of this condition as much as my mother was.

Not sure what this means, especially from that perspective. Why is it only that my mama was being pointed out? I'm not sure if it was the first, but it was one of many times I know I had an identity crisis. I was confused about who I was, and that the society we live in adds to the surface-level mindset of identity. What makes you normal anyway? When Grandma broke the news to tell me that Auntie Patti is not my mother, that was hard for me. That's where questioning myself about who I am, what my value is, and what the point of my life is all started for me.

So, it was like if my own parents—my mother and my father, the lady who carried me and the man whose sperm created me—didn't care or didn't want to stay around to be a part of my life. It made it hard to really comprehend that anybody else could genuinely love me. How you process what you take from your surroundings, how you try to learn from the things that are surrounding you. Take what benefits you from that experience, person, or thing.

Chapter 10

WHERE WERE YOU ON THE NIGHT OF?

Don't forget, we are solving a case, putting a puzzle together and adding color that will connect me to my history.

Sierra - "Sooooo, whose idea was it to split me and my sister up?"

Wanda - "I was dating a guy named Perry who lived in Sarasota at the time. Perry worked on a construction site. Your mom stayed with your dad at some boarding house. I went back to Sarasota shortly after your mom was supposed to move in with Momma. It wasn't too far from Ike's Liquor store off 12th Ave. Grandma still lived with Mr. Willie so your mama stayed there. Patti was in Tarpon Springs.

Your momma was not moving fast enough, I guess. Grandma called Patti and then me. I came over after work, we had the conversation about taking ya'll away from your mother because of her living situation. I decided to take Pokey because she was the youngest and Patty took you because you and Kimmy were close to the same age."

Not too long ago she said Darleen, but I corrected her. Darleen wasn't born at this time, and she disagreed with me. I told her it had to be Kimmie because Tony is older than me and Scrap and Snag are younger than me. So, it had to be Kimmie. I had to break it down by saying Kimmie is only a few months older than me, we are not even a year apart. Kimmie was born in April, and I was born in October in the same year, 1979.

I am loving all the color that is coming to this picture.

Sierra - "So, when did you move back in with grandma? I remember when we came to stay with Grandmother, you, Erica, and Pokey were already there."

Wanda blurted out, "Patti is not your Mama, Duke has always been your mother!" This was her way of zooming through the story.

In my normal squeaky, but most sarcastic voice I could stomach up, I said, "Auntie, of course, Duke is my mother. I am fully aware of that now! But why did nobody tell me that when I was younger?" I'm not sure why I never thought to ask this question. When is a good age to let a child know things like this? I had to step further outside of the box, outside of this being my own story, outside of this being my reality. I have mixed feelings and double mixed emotions when it comes to this topic.

I personally don't think there's a set age when you have this discussion with a child. It's situational, based on the happenstance surrounding it. Primarily based on the mental and emotional state of the child. My reasons for now asking why, this, or why that, was not to point any fingers or to find blame. I just found myself in a place much like the average child when they get to the phase where they ask why the sky is blue, why do birds fly, why is the grass green, why is my hair curly, where do babies come from, that stage.

This was by no means me looking to define something as right or wrong, I wanted to give my story color. I have learned that some people begged to differ. I've come to my own understanding that asking why or the need to have a story isn't to say whether it was good or bad, happy, or sad, but to live and experience, not create an identity from something that happened.

Once something has taken place, you get to decide what you will feel or think about that thing. Which, from my experience and from my journey, I have found it to be what I was missing. I have found it to be the colors that my canvas lacked. I have found it to be what feels like home. I found it to be the passkey to all that haunted me.

Much as a doorknob is still a door, much as a steering wheel is to a car, one could not be obtained without the other. One couldn't actually function to its fullest potential, to what it was designed to do, without the other.

I no longer add or take away anything that I have experienced thus far because I am now fully aware that, as Jim Carrey said, "Life doesn't happen to you, it happens for you."

I say I am right where I am supposed to be. I am currently the best version of myself, especially compared to what I was yesterday. I am currently no longer in what I felt was the longest battle with myself. I felt like I was going around and around the same mountain of uncertainty. Within me, looking at how the knowledge of these things has added a spectrum of color. I could've never created this picture with the 32 colors that currently existed in the crayon box. It has added so much to the person that I already was. I couldn't have seen it if I didn't take this rooted journey home. I can now fully appreciate, the one-of-a-kind masterpiece that I am and I can be in all the original masterpieces I will go down in history being. But back to where I left off in the interview.

I'll never know why my grandmother decided to tell me at the time she did. Would anyone else have told me if she hadn't? She knew that no one would tell me and that's why she took it upon herself to now ensure that I had knowledge of this two years before she died. As I said, she would always call us in her room one by one to give us some little sweet Debbie snack or something. She never had a particular order and when it was my turn that day, my yummy, yummy thoughts were dramatically changed.

I describe it like this, my exact words in my first book were, "This was the first time that I was able to express this to any family member in this manner." I told her how it played a big part in the made-up stuff that I told myself about myself and now knowing those things, I can allow the real Sierra to stand up. In some ways, on so many diverse levels, it was as if I was now daring myself to find out who I was and what I was made of.

It was a voice in me saying, to myself, "Wait till ya get a load of me." Although I didn't say that out loud, Wanda definitely had a perplexed look on her face. I assured her that I had not lost my mind, which allowed me to segue into letting her know what my first book *Finding Sierra* was all about. I told her it expresses what happened and what I learned from the experience. This is where I'm at now, I don't fight anybody. The parent or guardian can only give what they have experienced themselves.

I had now used this interview time to answer some of my own personal questions. I realized that I had a few questions I'd like to ask. Wow, that was so freeing to even type that because I didn't always have them. I mentioned this in *Finding Sierra* under the subtitle forever changed, talking about the experience of my grandparents dying in what seemed like a matter of days or weeks after each other.

I was able to ask Auntie Wanda exactly what the time span between the two deaths was and she said it was about six months.

I told her for a little girl, it felt like a matter of days. I told her it felt like I should not have been back at Smith Funeral Home so soon. She said my grandfather was in the hospital when this all took place with my grandmother. He made the decision to take her off the breathing machine. He was there for all of it, they wheeled him from his hospital room to where she was.

Wanda explained that the machine was turned off and since it was a respirator, it was breathing for her.

Wanda - "Once the machine was turned off, the reality of my mother dying became a real thing."

Sierra - "Where were you when you got the call about your father passing away?"

She said she would have to think about it because she was uncertain of her exact whereabouts when the news was brought to her.

Sierra - "Was he still in the hospital when he died or was he at home when he passed away?" (Making a mental note, to ask one of her siblings as well. One can clarify that a little more for me.)

I then told her of my experiences when talking with Uncle Desmond.

Sierra - "I noticed the signs of memory loss, is it dementia or Alzheimer's? I was uncertain. He spoke of Aunt Margie as if she were still living. When I first corrected him saying, 'No uncle, Aunt Margie has passed away.' He was aware of where she once stayed, yet was not aware she was no longer living. I didn't force this to be his reality, since being in the medical field for so many years, I welcome those times. I have my professional opinion, but I have my personal one also. Indulge them in what they do remember. I also know that people dealing with loved ones who suffered from either or both diseases deal with it differently."

Chapter 11

HARD PILLS CAN BE SWALLOWED

I do know that sometimes, being truthful about what your loved one is suffering from means that you must face the reality that your loved one now has these conditions. And sometimes, it's easier to not deal with it than to accept these facts. They equal to having a new normal, for sure! She was not as surprised about this as I thought she would be. She agreed and, in her rebuttal, said he is worse than me, which she is saying that she too suffers from one or the other.

This rooted journey home is dealing with what some would say is the elephant in the room. Again, it is a clear sign that we aren't cursed as families, we're just unlearned. I understand why it was a tradition to sit around campfires and tell stories in all forms, whether it was thorough words or songs. Songs are just stories with a melody. Songs are just words in the form of music notes. So much has changed between then and now and I am seeing obvious signs of these things. As I hear Kenny Chesney's song about tequila making her clothes come off playing in the background.

As my Grouper Reuben arrived at the table, Auntie Wanda was saying how she thought about moving to Madeira beach, but she didn't really like how things were just compact and on top of each other. You couldn't breathe she said. She remembers everything used to be right in the open. She didn't talk about how if a wave gets high enough, it's going to knock the buildings down.

Wanda - "I remember how horses used to walk up 54th Ave South, that's how open the area used to be."

So much has changed from her time from when she was younger to now. We then got on the topic again about my granddad. I was telling her that Darlene, which is Auntie Patty's youngest daughter, confirms her story. She shared that Granddad came here after World War One or something on the boat and never went back. She said she was unsure of which boat he came in on but the uniform he was in said he was from Great Britain. She says she's not sure about what happened. Was he trying to escape from his current life to find another one?

She was unaware of the complete details, and I laughed to myself because we have a cousin which I am looking to interview, Kenneth, who my uncle Desmond recommend I talk to.

Sierra - "Was he on America's Most Wanted list because he was coming in and out of the country when he wasn't supposed to be here?" I laughed and shook my head.

Wanda - "The FBI was even investigating the whole family at one time trying to figure out Kenneth's whereabouts."

So, they knew everything about the whole family, everybody's name was on the list. They knew down to the T where each family member worked. He kept the tradition going of having double-digit children. But she praised him because all his children were aware of one another.

This opened the floor for me to speak about how I felt about this from my own perspective. I wanted to have a bond with my sisters and my brothers. I confessed to her that it's still slightly challenging. It's not a conscious challenge, but it's a challenge. Obviously, something is there, because even though we have all expressed that we want to get to know each other, something is missing. Something stops it from happening.

When I think about it, Leroy didn't have the number of children he had. Yet this man made ensured his children knew one another as siblings. I strongly feel that as a man producing seeds, it's his right, his duty, to ensure that his offspring know of one another. This ensures that in a city as small as St Petersburg, no incest happens. We're as close as we say we desire to be despite his relationship with our mothers. They had nothing to do with us as children and now at an adult age, I'm just getting to know my sisters and brothers.

My heart gets a little heavy when I think about this because even with my purest intentions and the volume in the way that I love people, I find it slightly difficult to open myself up to my sisters. My brothers, not so much. But with those girls, it's a little more challenging. It was in the process of writing this book that I finally realized why. Innerstanding for me is finally here. If I can, let me fill you in.

So, last January my little sister, the youngest of us all, got married. She wanted all her sisters in her wedding, in spite of what some of the emotions could've been between everybody. I applauded her for this effort. I was honored to be in the wedding, yet I was worried. I remember saying to my friend that I was afraid something was going to pop off. I couldn't really put my finger on why I was strongly feeling this way.

We had to have meetings for bridesmaid stuff, such as rehearsals, where we all had to come together and meet up. These three or four meetings alone were the most time that I had been around all of them at the same time. Even during that time I still couldn't pinpoint why I felt like something was going to transpire. Now I look back and notice that although we hugged, smiled, and greeted one another, it was as if we were still separated into different groups.

Ok, so you have my oldest sister Angie, her mom is Sheila. That would be one group and the second group consisted of myself and my sister Shekina. The third group consisted of the bride-to-be, Kendra, and her sister Pookie. Did you notice how even when I was telling the story, I said hers and mine although we are all sisters because we come from the same sperm? The same seeds produced us.

It opened for me. It was as clear as when the clouds roll away on a cloudy day. I can see clearly now the rain is gone, and I am able to identify the obstacle that was hindering us, or hindering me, from completely accepting them or letting them in. Years prior to this, there were a few words shared between me and Kendra through Facebook. I read a post of hers where she mentioned her dad being here for the holidays and this was not the first time I saw this.

So, I direct messaged her. I left what I would call a nice but nasty message. Not directing it to her, but more so to Leroy, for him coming to St Pete, but not making it known to me or Nicole, my oldest sister. I don't know if she was even aware that he was in town. I refer to Nicole by her middle name. It's crazy that we were not afforded the same opportunity of knowing that our father was in town was my point.

Now the way she defended her father I couldn't even be mad at. I had my own fantasies of what it would be like to be a daughter. What it would be like to have an active father in my life. I applauded her for this, yet I was realistically bothered. She was defending a man who didn't play his role in making sure that his children got to know one another. How was he fine with coming into a city as small as St Pete and only visiting half of his children? Not affording the opportunity to all of us is what my message said.

She got so offended that she even threatened to fight me. Saying why didn't I see my dad or why was I not there in my father's life. I was slightly confused about this because I was the child. I, as they say, didn't ask to be born. I was a child, why was it my responsibility to ensure these things happened? Even still, the way my heart is set up, the way I am cosmically designed, I still put forth the effort as a teenager in middle school and in high school. Even after starting my adult life, I was always the one looking for Leroy.

I would hunt him down and it was always good for a week or two before he would fade away like the wind. By this time, I was tired of putting forth the effort into what seemed like a dead situation. The relationship didn't yield good fruit for me, so I stopped trying. My innerstanding was clear as a summer day. I realized why it was hard to let my sisters in. It was no longer due to my dad not being there. I have now been able to pinpoint it if you will.

Nicole and I's feelings around my father were always dismissed. Nicole has never hidden her feelings around our father. Sperm donor is what she calls him. Their experience with my father was different from ours. Although I could respect the fact that my father was in Kendra's life, she didn't afford me the same respect in understanding our reality or emotions about him.

Could this be the reason I felt like something was going to pop off during her wedding? I realized that I was preparing for an argument or a disagreement. I was ready to defend my space, finally! Usually, it was always Nicole speaking up about her feelings and her emotions towards our father. She didn't play nice, she didn't sugarcoat anything when it came to how she felt. I must admit that it hit me in a soft spot when I saw our father walk my little sister down the aisle.

Here Comes The Bride

I remember having a heated conversation with Nicole when I got married. She was upset with me because I wanted my dad to walk me down the aisle. I was adamant about this. She asked me a real question I was not ready for. "Why would you give him the opportunity to do that when he never was there for you?" She felt like I was shortchanging Jerry, who was my stepdad, as he had been around and dated my mom for the last 37 years.

Yes, he is my stepfather, but I wanted my dad to walk me down the aisle. What's so wrong with that, I asked. She couldn't wrap her mind around it nor was I trying to convince her. I guess I was still a daddy's girl without ever even having the daddy. Once my husband at the time and I went to pre-marriage counseling, I learned the meaning of the giving away of the bride, which made me reevaluate. I had to check myself. Leroy didn't deserve to walk me down the aisle. How do you give someone away when you don't even know them?

The giving away of the bride should feel like it comes at a cost. It should feel like you were letting go of something of value and turning it over to her husband to have and to hold. With this knowledge, I realized that Leroy didn't fit this mold, not because I didn't want my daddy to walk me down the aisle but because he didn't know the precious gift that I am. He had never wiped a tear from my cheek or comforted me. How could he even know the meaning of giving me away to my husband?

I didn't choose my stepdad either even though he and my mother had been together for so long. I'm not saying these things to say that it was a sad thing. It was, just what it was, so with all my new knowledge, I decided that my uncle Freddie (Desmond's best friend) would do the honors of walking me down the aisle. We had laughed, we had talked. I know how to bleed brakes, change oil, and flush my radiator because of him.

We used to take trips to the junkyard, which is my second favorite place to go. Home Depot is number one. So, I thought he deserved the honor of walking me down the aisle.

At my sister's wedding, I stood still, gazing towards the back of the room. As everyone stood to welcome the bride, as she entered the room, I saw my father on her arm and it gave me an uneasy feeling. Did I put this in my first book? The (M.U.S) about not having the father, daughter experience. I have questioned myself about so many different things about life. I remember being uncertain about a lot. One thing my heart is certain of is that I would've been a good daughter. If I'm honest with myself, a part of me always feels like I was robbed of this experience. I feel like this earthly experience should've been afforded to me.

I just know that I wouldn't have messed up being a daddy's girl. I know I would've gotten it right. I don't feel like I was able to do what I now define as adding color to my picture. This gave me the understanding of now being able to identify what has stood in the way of my bond with my sisters. Even though I feel so strong now, I haven't shared this with them yet, but I do anticipate doing so. I realized that it is a key factor in us having a relationship.

Chapter 12

QUANTUM LEAPING

At lunch with Auntie Wanda, there was a lady about three tables away from us that had on a happy birthday sash. She was sitting at the table with three other ladies, I told the bartender to ask her what she wanted to drink. I was going to take a shot with her for her birthday. Coincidentally, she went for tequila (me and Kimmie's drink). So when the server delivered the shots, she was taken aback by my gesture. We bit the lime and threw back the shot. Wanda and her table were in the background rooting us on. I had a brief discussion with the birthday girl and she revealed to me that the other three ladies at the table with her were her sisters. She said that she had seven sisters in total. I thought, how cool is that? It piggybacks on what I was saying to Auntie Wanda when we were talking about my cousin Kenny making sure that all his children were aware of one another.

I have no ill feelings towards Leroy. I am now able to say that. Never experiencing me as a daughter was his loss. Although I point more fingers at Leroy in the role that he chose to play as being a father.

Since I am being honest here about my experience and about my takeaway from this, I'll be honest about my disappointment with my father's wife. From our ages, you can obviously tell that my sister and I were born before the third group of children. My heart, being a woman too, isn't sure how she was ok with him showing up for her children but not his own children. I'm just expressing thoughts or questions that I never thought about or asked.

Although it's not your responsibility as a woman to force a man to see his kids, I don't understand how you can be with a man who doesn't take care of his responsibilities. It says a lot about her. AGAIN, MY OPINION! There's this saying I remember: children didn't ask to be born. I didn't ask to be here and if I remember correctly, history says that he was dating this lady while he was dating my mother. I have also heard rumors of there being more children outside of the ones that I know about to another girl. I cannot remember if she is older or younger than me.

I didn't just arrive at this conclusion solely off my emotions, I had the opportunity to be what you can call a stepmother. My chocolate bar is what I called him. He had two children when we got together. The baby mama was not happy in the beginning. She would call me out by name and was very disrespectful, yet I never played along or retaliated. I reminded myself that one thing I love about myself is how I face adversity. I can appear unbothered or I can make it my mission to put myself in other people's shoes.

I could completely understand her anger, hurt, disappointment, and the place she found herself in as a single parent. From that experience on top of knowing what it's like to not have a father present, I made it my business to ensure that these children who, again, didn't ask to be here, wouldn't have to feel what I felt about my stepmother. I never tried to take their mother's place so she saw that I was not there to replace her or to have him and not what came with him, meaning his children. So before that relationship was over, she and I became what I can say was friends and we were able to exchange numbers.

We would call each other often. We went school shopping every year for the babies. This was throughout my relationship with my chocolate bar, which was a little over six years. Our relationship continued, even when he went to jail for 23 months. Even with his physical absence, I still did all the things that we did when he was out. Letting the children stay over on the weekends. Picking them up from our club on the days that he was assigned. I now filled in for him in his absence. Although he could not be there, he and I were together as one. I knew what came with him, his children, who I loved.

We eventually broke up but what she and I did was something I can guarantee that adults in this time zone aren't doing. Handling the matter at hand maturely. With all those mixed emotions, I formulated the conclusion that my dad's wife also played a significant role in us not having a bond as siblings. When she agreed to love my father, that should have included us.

Auntie Wanda said not to blame her, then she started telling me some of her relationship stuff. She said that she was engaged three times.

Sierra - "What??? So what happened?"

Wanda - "It's bigger than just being married. It's a mental, physical, and emotional thing. The man has to be ready also. Plus, you got to listen to your own intuition."

She told me a man wanted to marry her, even when she was pregnant with Erica, her only child.

Sierra - "What was his name?"

Wanda - "His name was Edward. He wanted to marry me. He was headed off to the service and wanted to take us with him. Although it was not his child, he was still willing to sign up for the responsibility."

She says she turned down the opportunity to be with him and wasn't even 100% sure why. I shortchanged myself on so many things that were good opportunities because the perception I had of myself stopped me in my tracks. It hindered me with people who loved me for me and what I could bring to the table because I felt like what the person was desiring or needing from me, I couldn't give them.

So, I opted out of the relationship, situation, or whatever it was at that point exactly.

It was nice to hear her say she has no regrets in her life. She said she knows what it's like to love. She knows what it's like to have a broken heart. She knows what it's like to work hard for something and it still doesn't turn out the way you expected but she said she was able to be honest with herself, giving her the upper hand on anything that was brought her way.

Chapter 13

INTENTIONAL MINDSET

I had my mind made up, today was the day I was going to Syliva's house. She's the eldest niece of my grandfather, and since I missed the chance to speak to his last living sibling, Syliva would be the next in line. Now, I had said I was going to her house plenty of days before, yet still hadn't. But today, the thought that tomorrow may very well be too late, my mind was made up. I allowed myself the excuse of not really knowing the exact location, as to why it took me so long. That didn't change today either, but my thoughts did. I was going to find this house, TODAY!

I made it out of the house, questions in hand, excitement in my heart. I didn't have to travel far and halfway there, I felt the need to be outside, preferably under a tree. It was walk it out Wednesday in my Facebook group. The group encouraged members to do something intentional for themselves every day of the week. So, I decided to make a stop and gave myself a reason to be intentional about what I wanted to do. I paused for the cause and created an experience. It was a moment to be still, a moment to give thanks, a moment to reflect on what I was grateful for at the moment. I was prolonging this visit to see someone that was almost like a stranger although we shared ancestry and blood. I can't forget to mention that I still didn't really know where I was going.

I somehow knew not to panic because I told myself I was just going to drive right there and I admit, once I left the park, I gathered myself, and put my shoes back on. I did have to go around the block once because I didn't listen to myself the first time about the house that I thought was the house. I slowed down and took a deep, long stare at the porch, focusing on the structure of the building, trying to visualize if this was the house I remembered.

Sitting in the car wasn't going to answer my questions, so here we go. I grabbed my paper with my questions on it and locked the door. I walked up, knocked on the door and took a few steps back because of Covid-19. I had my mask on, she opened the door. I introduced myself as Sierra then asked if she knew me. She said yes and nodded politely before inviting me in. She was slightly amped up about the stove people being late delivering her new stove.

Sylvia - "Would you like some water?"

Sierra - "No, thank you."

With a slight gesture of her hand, she invited me to sit down.

I had several waves of emotions going on at the same time. Nervousness and thinking about what to say now that I was here. Does she really know who I am? I can see the resemblance between my grandfather and her mother, Margie. One of the emotions took over, and before I knew it, I said, "So, Duke is my mother, so that means my grandfather is your brother?"

Cutting me off, she strongly said, "UNCLE."

Sierra - "So, I'm writing a book about my granddad. But I also want to talk about things that happened around St. Pete during those times. So, it's going to be *like a small history book about St. Pete but a closer look at the roots I'm growing from. My little cousins that come after me never saw my grandfather, all we have is stories about him. I like those glasses on you. Like, those are nice.*

At some point, they might want to know who their grandfather, great-granddad, and great uncle are too. So, I thought that I would write this book to help answer some of those questions that we might have about him. I spoke to Desmond and he suggested that I see you because you're nice, so here I am.

So, you're my mom's first cousin then...right?"

Sylvia - "Brother and sister's children."

Sierra - "Right, right. As all of this starts coming together for me, it's weird when you think of us being children. You don't think of your parents as having a first cousin, you just think, oh, that's your mom. So, the idea that she had cousins feels weird."

Sylvia - "A whole slew of them."

I feel like I needed to get right to the questions as she doesn't seem to be a woman of many words.

Sierra - "Ok, so who was your mom?"

Sylvia - "Pearl, um Pearl was the oldest sister...the oldest child."

Sierra - "Ok, so give it to me this way, how many were there?"

She started naming them off the top of her head, starting with Pearl.

Sylvia - "It was Pearl, Violet..."

Sierra - "Oh, I remember Violet."

Sylvia - "William, which was Barbara's father, we used to call him Bill. Author, Marjorie, your granddad, Hugh, and then Lucille. Lucia was the last child. There were seven alive, but there were 13 children in all. The others didn't make it. She had a set of twins that died."

Sierra - "And this is my granddad's mom?"

Sylvia - "Yes."

Sierra - "What was her name?"

Sylvia - "Eliza."

Sierra - "Ooh, that's who my mom is named after. (I said in that high-pitched voice I have when I get excited.) She's mentioned proudly to me a few times being named after her grandmother."

Sylvia - "Eliza Brooks-Lord."

Now that I'm typing, I realize I should've asked for the correct spelling of the name because my mom mentioned to me before how they changed the spelling of her name. Auntie Wanda, as well.

Sierra - "So where did Burgess come from?"

Sylvia - "Burgess was your grandfather's name. The first five children were Lord."

Sierra - "So, in talking to Auntie Wanda to get information for the book, she herself realized she doesn't know much about my grandmother's parents. She didn't even know if my grandmother had sisters and brothers."

INTENTIONAL MINDSET

Sylvia - "Well, when your grandmother met my uncle, most of her siblings were old. I knew Aunt Alice and Uncle James."

The fact that she was able to give me names blew my mind.

Sierra - "So, it was Alice James?"

Sylvia - "The oldest sister was Alice and then Uncle James came in after because I think he was after Granny. Then Aunt Esther and Uncle Albert."

Sierra - "Oh wow, Auntie Wanda didn't mention any of these names."

The plot thickens, I thought as I scratched my head with the edge of my pen like a real detective.

Sylvia - "She never knew. She knew nothing about them. She wasn't born or was too young."

Sierra - "How did my grandma my granddad meet in Florida?"

She had a perplexed look on her face. I don't think she heard exactly what I said so I repeated it slowly, "My grandmother and grandfather, where did they meet?" Her eyebrows went up and she had a smirk on her face.

Sylvia - "He came from Belize, joined the service and at some point, he met Nora."

Sierra - "So there's a story that my grandmother found him on the railroad tracks because he didn't get back on the ship to go where he was supposed to go."

Sylvia - "I don't know that to be true, all I know is he met her and they lived together. I don't know if they ever really got married."

Sierra - *"I remember it correctly because Desmond mentioned it when I interviewed him."*

Sylvia - *"Yes, they stayed together and so they were under that common law marriage thing. Those days common-law marriage counted. Nora had a son from another guy when he met her."*

Sierra - *"Yes, my uncle Larry. So, was Larry young when my grandfather came into the picture?"*

She said yes with a little excitement. Then she started naming off the list of the kids: *"Wanda, Desmond, your mother, Patti, then Chantay."*

Sierra - *"You know all this time I thought my mom was older than Uncle Desmond, but he happily clarified that when I interviewed him."*

Sylvia - *"No, no, no, Desmond, was the second child. It's Desmond then your momma."*

We had a moment of silence as I processed everything that was being said while my brain started filing all this information away.

Sierra - *"So how many children did Pearl have?"*

Sylvia - *"Two."*

So, I just started going down the list of my grandfather's siblings. Violet, Normand, and William. She looked to the sky and said oh lord. I chuckled at her. She went to name them off softly as if she was provoking the thought out of hiding.

Sylvia - *"There was Pinky, Geroge, William, Wayne, Barber, Sandra, Cliffton, and Terrace. There was a total of nine children, that I know of, besides who they lost in-between. And then Author, he had five children. Three girls and two boys."*

INTENTIONAL MINDSET

Sierra - "Then what about Margorie?"

Sylvia - "She had only one. Lucila had five."

Sierra - "My grandfather also had five children."

Brain processing...as the color is loading.

Sierra - "And who is your mother, did you tell me?"

I answered before she could and said Margorie? Sylvia said no and waited a few seconds before she answered my question.

Sylvia - "Pearl is my mother..."

Me sitting quietly as the color filled in the picture of my history, loading...

Sierra - "So that means you're the oldest niece from the oldest child..." Download complete!

"Yes!" She said with a slight sound of excitement in her voice as if she too saw the DOWNLOAD COMPLETE notification.

Sierra - "Awwwwww, I see why they told me to talk to you. You're the oldest niece of the oldest child. I needed to talk to you because you know all the information. So, you're like the mother to all the other little cousins. Ok so, what part of the family lives in Chicago? How does Chicago come into the picture?"

Sylvia - "Pinky's children live in Chicago. That's Barbara's sisters and brothers and those are Bill's children. Bill's grandchildren and great-grandchildren live in Chicago. They're all from Pinky."

Chapter 14

THEY CAN TELL BY THE WAY I WALK, I AIN'T FROM AROUND HERE

Sierra - *"So, tell me about Belize, what did you do there?"*

Syliva - *"I taught at school."*

Sierra - *"What was the name of the school you graduated from?"*

Syliva - *"I went to an all-girls school, then I went to high school. I came here in 1963."*

Sierra - *"Wanda mentioned the elementary, the middle, and the high schools being all together at one time. So that's why I was asking, just to compare the school system."*

Sierra - *"When I was talking to Desmond, he said he was a migrant, so when my granddad was here, did he visit quite often because they brought the* sisters here? Is that how that went? Did he go back to Belize, once he came to Florida?"

Sylvia - "He never went back home."

Sierra - "Never went back home! Oh, wow."

Sylvia - "Lucille came here in 1962. She stayed for a while. I don't know what happened to Trump. He came and stayed with them for a while, and I guess things didn't work out. So, he moved out. That was so stupid at that time. When your granddaddy dated her, she lived in the projects."

Sierra - "Where they build the Sun Dome stadium, right?"

Sylvia - "Yes. I cannot remember the name, but that's when he debuted that he bought the house on Union Street. I remember when he bought the house because we lived on 13th Street. On Sundays, your granddad used to take his children to church. Rather, they used to go to traveler's rest, right?"

Sierra - "I didn't know my granddaddy went with them. I remember my grandma making sure me and my little cousins went every Sunday. We would most Sundays, it was just up the hill on the corner. Across the street on the opposite corner was Carters Flower shop. Both of these landmarks are currently in the same location."

THEY CAN TELL BY THE WAY I WALK, I AIN'T FROM AROUND HERE

Sylvia - "Your granddad took them to church, not your grandma. Your grandma didn't go."

Sierra - "How long have you lived here?"

We paused for a second because she was having a stove delivered. She was making a phone call because she missed the call, but I told her that I didn't hear the telephone ring while I was sitting there waiting.

We talked about how you don't know how much trash goes under the stove until you actually move the stove. She said you couldn't keep trash under that stove, but it was the splashing of food particles that she needed to clean up around the stove itself.

She was saying that if the caller didn't leave a message, they obviously didn't want anything

I asked again, "So how long have you lived at this address?"

She started humming this sweet little tune to herself and her eyes looked up in her head to do the math.

Sylvia - "I've been here 51 years, moved in 1971."

Sierra - "Wow, that's older than me. What was the area like when you moved in 50 years ago?"

Sylvia - "It was a mixed crowd. It was mixed with African American people and white people."

Suddenly the location of her house dawned on me. It was located not too far from Food Lion where my grandmother passed away. It was literally across the street from where she currently stays. So, I mentioned that to her after doing some math of my own.

Sierra - "That means you stayed here when my grandmother passed away in Food Lion."

Sylvia - "I was in this exact house when I got the phone call about Nora. She didn't die in the store. She died when she got to the hospital."

Although I could hear everything, I looked up and noticed the guys handling the stove. I was very intrigued about how they took it back out to the truck. I think she noticed the expression on my face, and she too had stopped talking to watch.

They didn't use a dolly, they had straps on their back, and something went under the stove. They lifted the whole entire, thing. So, one man was on each side to carry the stove. I thought that way was neat. Less stressful on the body. The name of the lady that my grandfather now lives with, Authorly, popped into my mind.

Sierra - "Wanda said she remembers asking her father when he was coming back home and he said when your momma gets younger. So, she knew he wasn't coming back home because she knew her mother couldn't get any younger. This new lady that he was currently dating was a younger woman."

Sylvia spoke with a smile on her face, much like Uncle Desmond did when he had a fond memory of my grandmother going out dancing.

Sylvia - "Your grandfather was always a sharp dresser, always. He always dressed extremely nicely with a hat to match his shoes, and a suit to match. He was always debonair. Head to toe."

I asked her if she knew the time span between the two passing away because I told her it seemed like it was only a day or a week that went by before we got the news that my grandfather was no longer here. Wanda said it was like six months and Cousin Silvio said It was longer than six months. I needed to find this information out, which I planned on doing.

THEY CAN TELL BY THE WAY I WALK, I AIN'T FROM AROUND HERE

So, when I look up the obituaries of the two, I will be able to tell from the date printed on each obituary the time span between the two deaths.

I started telling her my side of the story about me being 11 years old when my grandmother passed away and she said to me because I was a child, it felt that way to me. She said my grandfather was not sick and he died in the hospital.

But she said the woman died before my grandmother died, the side chick that is, so my grandfather lost both of his girls. He lost his main chick and the side one. My grandfather left my grandmother for a younger woman and my grandmother put him out when she found out about this other woman. He went to stay with his sister for a little while and then he moved out from there.

It was after the separation from my grandmother that he started buying different properties, like the building that the city of St. Petersburg now knows as the Hugh Burgess estate. Sylvia brought to my memory that Authorly and her children lived in that upstairs apartment in the back where at one point, Uncle Freddy used to fix cars.

It was when I was talking to Eric Atwater that he refreshed my memory of who this lady was. I remember them from when I was younger. So, when my grandmother had her incident in a Food Lion, my grandfather was already in the hospital. She said my grandmother had a stroke. I thought it was a brain aneurysm but she said it was a stroke.

"Oh, they didn't put the table back," she randomly blurted out. Referencing back to the guys delivering the stove. I told her I could help her if she needed me to. She was saying how everything was a mess because they just finished painting and they took things down.

She came back from the kitchen and sat back in a recliner. She hit the button and put her feet up. Then she went in about the guy from two weeks ago who was supposed to come back to put the carpet down but hasn't come back yet. She says she found someone else to put the carpet down. So, I continued my story. I started telling her about this day from the eyes of an 11-year-old girl. There was a knock on the door, it was Ms. Willoughby. I was concerned because I didn't see my grandmother. Where are the groceries that I was supposed to help put away? I went back to my business, then I remember the house filling up with people later.

But I don't recall what happened next. I'm still uncertain about whether they told everybody that grandmother passed away or what really happened, but my grandmother didn't come home. Sylvia said my grandmother didn't die right away, they took her to the hospital and she died there. This is similar to what Wanda said when I interviewed her. She said my grandfather was in the hospital when this incident happened.

At that point, my grandmother was on a ventilator, and they waited for my grandfather to come to her bedside to discuss whether they were going to take her off the ventilator or not. Sylvia said she cannot confirm nor deny if my grandfather was in the hospital at that moment, but she said that he was sick with kidney problems. In every picture of him, he looked like a healthy young lad. He looked like the extremely healthy, muscular Bill that I knew. I can't imagine him having kidney failure.

He worked for the school system for a long time, even while driving himself back and forth to dialysis, when he still could. She talked about my grandfather's mother living here for quite some time with Margie off of 3rd Ave. She said they would rotate her between the children until she died at Violet's house on Saturday morning, December 19th. They were living by 22nd Street where Perkins had bought up all that property.

Slyvia - "There was a huge fire in Belize in 1951. The fire went from one side of the island to the other. 13 families got burnt out, it was the worst fire we ever had. I was about 10 or 11 years old. I remember going to my Uncle Bill's house saying, 'Fire, fire!' that's all I could say because I was so shocked."

THEY CAN TELL BY THE WAY I WALK, I AIN'T FROM AROUND HERE

Sierra - "Wow, wow," that's all I kept saying.

Sylvia - "Your granddad was in the service, that's why we got to stay in America."

Sierra - "I was given information about how my grandparents originally met. He didn't get back on the boat. My grandmother was with Larry's father when they found him on the railroad track. The story says, my grandfather had on a uniform."

Sylvia - "He was here from 1948 or something like that. I don't know what he served in."

Sierra - "Everyone I talked to is unsure about that also. So, this is something I need to research to find the information (color) behind it. That way, it can reveal the history of this fantastic being, my grandfather."

Sylvia - "Your mother's mother lived there on 3rd Ave on Royal Court. I remember she too died suddenly. How's Desmond doing?"

Sierra - "He was the first person I interviewed. He's alright, but his mind is going. I believe it's dementia." I answered but she kept right on talking.

Sylvia - "I don't know what he ranked and how far he had gotten. When I came to Florida, he was working for the school system. He and I worked for the school for about 10 years. I was a teacher."

Sierra - "I must find out because we don't know if he was in the marines or the navy. At this point, we don't know any of that. So, I must figure that part out. I'm sure they have records of it somewhere. Desmond even told me Margie was still alive. He instructed me to see Margie as she would know more than he would. Correcting him one time I said, 'Uncle, she is no longer with us.' But he insisted that Margie was still living, pointing in the direction of where she last lived on that brick road, right there on the corner. It was up the street and around the way from where we used to do the family picnics in the yard under the big oak tree."

Here Are Your Flowers

We lost Uncle Desmond before his birthday, after the interview...

Sylvia - *"Desmond will be 70 in October, so that will make Wanda what, 71 or 72?"*

Sierra - *"He is right across the street from Melrose Elementary School."*

Sylvia - *"I know, Kenneth said 15th Ave somewhere. When I saw him the last time, I said, 'Oh my God, he has no teeth in his mouth.'"*

I busted out laughing because like sister, like brother.

THEY CAN TELL BY THE WAY I WALK, I AIN'T FROM AROUND HERE

Sierra - "My mom didn't like to wear her teeth either. When I went to interview Wanda, she had gotten all her teeth pulled as well. So, she was also snag-toothed."

Slyvia - "I don't know if they're married now."

Sierra - "They are married. She's his second wife."

Slyvia - "I didn't know that! I don't remember him having married anybody else."

Sierra - "I don't know all the details. Just that his first wife passed away. She was a friend or a family member helping out after things transpired. Once her mouth reopened from lockjaw."

Slyvia - "I don't know! What's her name, Desiree, right? Oh my God, Desmond is looking more like Nora."

Sierra - "I so agree, he's definitely looking more like my grandmother the older he gets. He has moles on his face, just like my grandma did. I've noticed that a few of the women in the family, including me, do as well."

Come to think about it, I felt like I was the one being interviewed now.

Sylvia - "How is Patti?"

Sierra - "She's doing as good as expected. She just had a birthday, so we took her on the boat. We made the most of it, it was hard for her not having Kimmie there."

Sylvia, cutting me off - "Yeah, I know Patti, Chantay and your momma are all born in February."

Sierra - "My mom's birthday is February 9th, Patti's the 19th, and Chantay's is the 28th. My mom is 65, I think."

Sylvia - *"Speaking of her, how is your mother?"*

Sierra - *"My mom is doing exceptional. She and my stepfather still have their apartment. His health is declining, so she's been living a new normal."*

Sylvia - *"Where does she live at?"*

Sierra - *"She's off 7th and 7th Ave North. Over there by that Save a Lot and Walgreens, back that way. They've been there for a few years now since she has gotten clean. Since my stepfather had those few strokes, he cannot move his right side and is no longer talking in complete sentences. Just a lot has changed. He's now incontinent, he doesn't move like he used to. We have the diapers and stuff but just so he can move around in his wheelchair more freely. I would like to get them a bigger space, but it costs more money. But they have enough between the two of them, they can afford it, so we are working on a plan. She's doing good, she's still holding it down and is still off drugs and alcohol."*

Slyvia - *"What about Chantay? The daughter that used to live with Wanda?"*

Sierra - *"She's all grown up with children of her own, she has three babies now. We just got together on Chantay's anniversary in the alley behind Atwater's to celebrate her life. This time, all her grandkids were there,"* I say as I show her a picture on my phone.

"This is Joe, Chantay's oldest son, and this is Chantay's other son, Linwood. And in this picture, you have her children, except the oldest daughter lives out of town."

Sylvia, interrupting me - *"Is that the girlfriend?"*

Sierra - *"No, that's me!"* I said. Moving on to the next photo, *"This is me taking a picture with all of them. This is Linwood, which is Chantay's son, they got the call and they had to go somewhere down to Miami to pick him up."*

THEY CAN TELL BY THE WAY I WALK, I AIN'T FROM AROUND HERE

Sylvia - *"That was Chantay's first child. Yeah, I remember the call. He was such a fat baby. Oh, I remember that fat baby."*

Sierra - *"He was definitely a chunky something, he had those rolls in his elbows and knees. Although Chantay had two children before he was born."*

Slyvia - *"I don't know a quarter, much less half of the children. I've never seen them."*

Sierra - *"I know that's how I feel, which is the reason I'm writing this book, so it can be like a family tree for all of us. The point of me wanting to do the book is so we can merge the family together."*

Slyvia - *"There's a crowd in Chicago with their children and then all their children, and their children."*

Sierra - *"Right, you said it was Bill's side of the family that was up there."*

Sylvia - *"Yes, you have Terrace, Sandra, and Clifton. Sandra has two children, Beverly has four children, Clifton has about four children. Bev's live here with Barbara, and he has one child. His name is William, but we call him Bev's. He's in the hospital right now."*

Sierra - *"Oh no, I'm sorry to hear that."*

Sylvia - *"He had Covid. He's in Saint Anthony's Hospital right now."*

She gave me the complete rundown on the children's children, she knew her stuff.

Sylvia - *"You also have Pinky's children Marshall, Anna, Paulette, and Deon. There's a lot of them up there. She called them yellow people. You know Margie, you know Violet. Author was here at some point but only stayed about a year, he didn't like the American style."*

Sierra - *"So, is there anyone in Belize that is first- or second-generation?"*

Sylvia - *"Eddie died but there are some people in Belize, they had children. They ought to be a good age right now. Next year I'll go to Belize."*

Sierra - *"Well, if you think about going, will you include me because I would love to go, and it will be nice to go with someone who has been there before."*

Sylvia - *"Maybe some of Granny's sisters' children, children (referring to my grandfather's mother) are still there."*

Sierra - *"The Chicago side I'm ready to meet. This year, in honor of Kimmie, Patty's daughter who passed away, I'm doing a fundraiser. So, we're going to have a person out talking about life insurance and just other different things to empower the community. I'd just like to bring awareness to certain things that will disrupt the conversation around death. Also, there will be a financial advisor and we're going to talk about writing wills and those kinds of important things. We must start talking about these things in families cause we don't talk about them often. We're living as if we don't know that at some point, somebody's going to die.*

We don't know when or we don't know where, but we're not preparing. We're out here living like we don't know it's going to happen. Death is something that's guaranteed to be an experience in a family. So, I just want us to be as ready as we can be for the next time it happens. It could be me next time."

Sylvia - *"Was she sick?"*

Sierra - *"I heard rumors of her having lupus, which is a little form of cancer from my understanding."*

Slyvia - *"Did she have children?"*

THEY CAN TELL BY THE WAY I WALK, I AIN'T FROM AROUND HERE

Sierra - "She had one son, Equilyes. I noticed a change in Kimmie. All of a sudden, she just started really losing weight. She didn't complain of pain, at least not to me. She was serious about her privacy, she doesn't really let you in. Patti was upset because she talked to her every day and still didn't know."

Sylvia - "So, her mother didn't even know, she didn't tell her mother?"

Sierra - "Yeah, that's what I said too. Tony is Patti's oldest boy. Patti has five children, three boys and two girls. Tony's been married now for a long time, like double-digit years. He's been working and doing really well. I don't know if they bought the house, but they've been there for quite some time."

I was doing a very crappy job at explaining to her exactly where he lives. My friend Brian often tells me how directionally challenged I am. I think I proved him right. She definitely knew her city better.

Sierra - "If I'm going this way, then that street is 14th but then after that, it becomes Queens Borough."

Sylvia - "Is it a new house or an old house?"

Sierra - "I think it's an older house. You have 37th so it must be going further up on 37th or 38th. When you go up that street, you can't go straight so it might be 38th Street and 14th Ave, so he lives in between 37th and 38th off 15th Ave, right on the corner. I know it's a Jamaican man, he has his garden planted over that way. He's been working for some company for a little while now. I don't know exactly what he does. Tony has children, but his children are older as he had them before he got married."

Sylvia - "How is Patti's little boy?"

Sierra - "Oh you mean Patti's son, from marriage, Lo'? He just turned 13 the other day. I stopped by Patti's house to talk about the Blue Lips, Don't

Care event and ended up with a car full of children going to Sky Zone for his birthday."

Lo' has been having a hard time with school and this is his first death experience. He might need somebody to talk to, like these things, they mess with you. Like when my grandmother passed away, it messed with me.

Chapter 15

LET'S TALK ABOUT DEATH, CAN WE?

The thing is that no one sat down to talk to me about death. Nobody really said to me, "Your grandmother isn't coming back." It was like a week or so later that I realized that grandma wasn't coming back through the door.

I was looking for her to come back but I only saw the neighbor's car coming and going and I wondered where she was. Nobody really explained that to us. So, I believe Lo' is experiencing that.

Sierra - *"Yes, I told Patti she has to talk to him. These are things that need to be talked about in families. These are the topics that I want to cover in the event I'm doing in honor of Kimmie. I'm hoping to disrupt our thoughts, feelings, and emotions on the elephants in the room. We aren't generationally cursed as a people, we're just generationally unlearned. I want to change this narrative for my family. I want to have a tighter-knit family for my little cousins so they don't have to experience how a lack of communication can stifle their ability to grow.*

It's hard now because Lo' was at Kimmie's house every weekend. It's a whole new normal that he must get used to. Kimmie baked him a cake every year, so now when these birthdays are coming along, and those things are not happening, it's a reminder for him that Kimmie is not here.

I grew up thinking Kimmie and Tony were my brother and sister. I thought Patti was my Mama."

Slyvia - "But Patti's not your mother!"

Sierra - "I didn't know that, I had no idea until my grandma told me. This was life-altering information. I refer to this in my first book as my first identity crisis."

It seems that as children, you're supposed to know what's not being shown and understand what's not being said.

As I am typing this, I wonder if she hadn't told me, who was going to tell me? How long would they let me believe that Patti was my mother, and her husband was my father? Again, I'm back to my original point, this is why it's important that families talk about the elephants in the room. We hide things from our children and we cover things up, not discussing and sharing, as if one day, your babies won't grow up and have thoughts of their own and be able to see through the generational uncommunicated things in the family.

This brings tears to my heart and my heart cries because there are topics about incest, molestation, and more that have gone undiscussed. There are cries out for help that went unheard. While families passed down family secrets, we're unknowingly passing down unlearned behavior. News flash, your children will do exactly what you do, they will carry that with them in some form or fashion so can we abandon the thought around do as I say not as I do. That concept has done its own injustice in mentally enslaving us.

You can die, emotionally and mentally as well as physically. Everybody started

LET'S TALK ABOUT DEATH, CAN WE?

treating me differently, like instantly when they found out who my mother was. My mother was a crackhead and I didn't know who my daddy is.

I didn't even know Shekina was my sister. When Shekina and I found out we were sisters, there was so much pain around the whole idea that I feel we still haven't recovered from. What's a child to do??

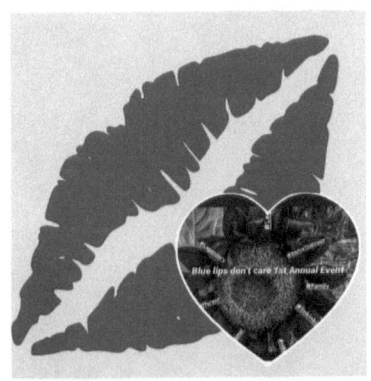

My Favorite Uncle

I arrived at Barbara's house with the same excitement, as my uncle Desmond. Barbara is my grandfather's niece. Barbara's father and my grandfather are brothers. When I got out of the car, I heard a faint voice saying..."Come around the back, I'm back here." I started towards the backyard and she greeted me with a smile. She told me to have a seat, pointing to the patio furniture to the right. She said, "I'm just in the back cleaning up all these leaves and branches that have fallen from the trees. Beeves, (our cousin) will be out soon to give me a had."

Sierra - "Can I help you?"

LET'S TALK ABOUT DEATH, CAN WE?

Babara - "No thanks. Take a seat," she said, pointing in the direction of the patio furniture.

She said Tammy (real name Tammara) would be here Saturday.

"This Saturday, coming?" I asked with a smile on my face.

Tammy and I met for the first time a few months back. Her mom and my mom are first cousins, so that makes us second cousins. We jammed right away, she's such a sweet soul. We talked for hours like we had known one another all our lives. We discussed me coming to Chicago, but it seemed she was making her way here before I could head her way.

Barbara - "Because my birthday is coming up and she told me she's gonna take me to my favorite place when she gets here."

Sierra - "What place is that?"

Barbara - "The casino!"

Beeves came round the corner, talking junk about the leaves, the ones she was just fussing about also. She looked over at me and said, "You can ask all the questions you want to ask."

She has a genuinely nice backyard. 'Are those mango trees,' I inwardly questioned as I slowly scanned, taking in the view. She walked towards the east end of the yard. She noticed a turtle nest and said, "This is the time of year that they came up and dig holes in the backyard for the eggs." She had a little barricade around it to ensure nobody accidentally trampled over it. Then, she went back fussing.

Barbara - "I didn't want to pay for the dumpster, it's way too much money. So, I decided every week, I'll load the garbage can and the recycling bin with the branches and the leaves to get rid of them that way."

Sierra - "Ok, so let's start with the questioning, who was Hugh Burgess to you?"

Barbara - "He was my uncle. I remember that he visited us in Chicago when we lived there."

Sierra - "Were you little?"

Barbara - "I wasn't that young. He brought Otha Lee up there with him. She was a nice lady."

She started rejoicing at the fact that this was the last round of bins they had to load. Helping her to rejoice, I told her that it was motivating, cause she can scratch that chore off the list. I smiled to myself because this was something that I had started implementing in my life as I was starting to monetize and organize this amazing life of mine.

Sierra, mumbling to myself as I wrote the notes - "Ok, so he was your uncle."

She must've heard me because she replied stating, "Yes, he's my father's brother."

Barbara - "He was my Indian uncle."

Sierra - "Indian?"

Barbara - "I think so. I heard stories about this, plus he had the curly hair."

Sierra - "So Barbara, what's your father's name?"

Barbara - "William."

Sierra - "They call him Bill, right?"

Barbara - "Yes."

LET'S TALK ABOUT DEATH, CAN WE?

I smile because I'm adding color to this picture more and more.

Sierra - "I heard a lot about Mr. Bill. He's the one that's located in Chicago, right?"

Barbara - "Yes, you have a bunch of cousins in Chicago you've never even met yet."

Sierra - "I'm trying to get up there to see the Chicago family. I would love that to be a part of the book, even if it's just downloadable audio or footage that I can record."

Barbara - "Beverly has four children, Kimmie, Venard, Sheena and Monique."

All I heard was Kimmie. My ears perked up like a dog hearing a dog whistle. That was shocking because Patti's daughter's name is Kimmie.

Sierra - "How do you spell her name?"

MY heart was beating fast because I was not expecting her to say that; it threw me off guard.

Barbara - "K.I.M.M.M.I.E, I think I'm correct I have the right spelling on the inside."

Sierra - "I just was curious because I wanted to know if she spelled it the same way as my Blue Angel."

Barbara shouted to Beevs (they are first cousins) as he walked to the front side of the house, "Will you unlock the back door so we don't have to walk all the way to the front when we were ready to go in?"

She didn't want to walk back around to the front of the house. She wasn't happy about the sand being on her feet. She then commented about how she hated the fact that when she was out in public, she could see people with slippers on and the bottom of their feet are dirty. It drove her crazy. She mumbled to herself, "I'm losing so much weight I'm losing everything."

Sierra - "So Beverly is your sister, and she had four children?"

I was backtracking to help ground myself back to where I was going.

Sierra - "How many children did you have?"

Barbara - "I didn't have any, I was too busy working. I just helped out when I could."

I call this being part of the village, so I know that she too was helping raise the children in the family although she didn't birth them.

Barbara - "I worked too much, too damn much. They all send me Mother's Day gifts and stuff, it's nice. I've been in nursing for 39 and a half years."

Sierra - "So, did you graduate from nursing school in Chicago or..."

Before I could get the full sentence out, she was replying to me.

Barbara - "Yes, in Chicago."

Sierra - "You said you had a birthday coming up, how old will you be?"

Barbara - "68."

She was just dumping so much information, I didn't know what to do with it. The question that broke the levy was, "How many siblings did you have?"

Barbara - "Too many. You have Clearance, Rita, Pinky, George, William, Wayne—he passed away—then me, Sandra, Clifton, Beverly, and Teresa. Sandra *has two kids, Tamaran and Tyrone who are brother and sister.* Teresa has three kids, Shayla, Dominique and Darius."

She said it again, "Tammra is actually going to be here Saturday."

Sierra - "Oh, that would be cool because my book signing is this Saturday."

Her head turned as if it was on a swivel and said, "Book?"

Sierra - "Yes, it's my first book. I'm interviewing you now for the second book."

Barbara - "So, what's the first book about?"

Sierra - "Just a book about my life and how I took the things that happened to me and made it all work for my good."

I looked in my bag to see if I had a book so I could show her, but I didn't have any at that moment.

Barbara - "And now you are writing one about your family."

Sierra - "Yes," I replied with so much excitement in my voice.

I just felt like she understood the reason writing the book was important.

Sierra - "You are exactly right. I realized, how do we know where we're going if we don't know where we come from?"

Barbara - *"Yeah, because we are Belizean. You're Belizean and American so you can get two passports. I think we're considering going home next year."*

Sierra - *"Please let me know this information so I don't miss out on this trip. It's a must that I get there."*

Barbara - *"I haven't seen Patty in a while."*

Sierra - *"She's doing ok. She's currently in Pennsylvania with her middle child. Visiting, or more so, being introduced to their second child. We just got back from Puerto Rico, her youngest child Darleene turned 21. So, we went there to celebrate her birthday with her."*

It was me, Patti, Darleene and one of her college friends. Us being together made me aware of just how much we look alike. I've been noticing lately that I can look at a picture of myself and see a resemblance to the women in my family. Bypassing our sizes and skin being the same complexion.

It has to be something in my genetic makeup because it's a question I get asked often. I guess it's clear by the way I walk, talk, or just my demeanor that I ain't from around here. I'm only second generation in St. Petersburg, FL. Some of my friends are 4th and 5th generation and I guess this is more noticeable than I gave it credit.

This is interesting because I used to get questioned and still do to this day. Sometimes people wonder where I'm from and I tell them that I was born and raised in Saint Pete, but they say that I don't talk like it.

Sierra - *"I need to get to Belize, I need to get there. I knew granddad was from Honduras."*

Barbara - *"Belize,"* she said in a stern voice. *"Honduras is Spanish behind us and Mexico is on the other border. There is Honduras, Mexico, and San Salvador above, and then there's something else I can't remember."*

LET'S TALK ABOUT DEATH, CAN WE?

Sierra - "I heard through the grapevine that my grandfather spoke French and Spanish."

Barbara - "Uncle Hugh was in the army in England with my daddy and then I think he came to America and joined the army."

Sierra - "This is the reason why I'm even writing a book because I want to expound on how this man who wasn't even from America came here and established so much. This is why I titled it A Rooted Journey Home. I want to write this book because I want to honor my grandfather and boast about how what you could call an immigrant, came to America, became the bridge for his family to join the Land of the Free, earned a living, planted his own seeds to start his family, and bought land. I want to ensure that we save the last property. I don't understand how they have all just let it go down the pipe.

The reality is, it's not my place to make sure that they preserve what their father left them. Their dad pushed against the odds to ensure he left something better for his family. The Hugh Burgess estate consisted of five properties, each child could've had a piece of land and a house of their own. This was an era where people who looked like my grandfather didn't come by these things so easily, nor were people just giving land away. In reality, people were still being killed for the color of their skin, families were being evicted, tribes were being removed, and Indians were lied to and slaughtered just to get land."

Sierra - "Do you remember Sophia? She was a woman of the night. My granddad used to give her money and stuff, and at one point, he even gave her a place to stay. That apartment that was in between the big brick house and the duplexes."

Barbara - "That's a lot of building they lose. Your granddad owned lots of property."

I found myself feeling like I was carrying this burden of wanting to keep the last property. I'm just the granddaughter who would love to ensure that this property remains in the family. It could be a bank account, it could be a way to produce and create generational wealth.

If we play our cards right, this could bless our children for generations. We're currently battling with the city of St Petersburg as they have come with a fine from 20 years ago that said they've been charging us $100 a day. They want to take the property away from us. The property that their father wanted them to have. He left it to his children and, at one point, there was definitely land available for each child to obtain family wealth for each of their children.

Sierra - "Do you know about my granddad's father and mother?"

Barbara - "I know about granny, I know a lot about granny. Well, no as I think about it, I don't know that much. We have very beautiful women in our family. Granny, your grandad's mother, had a lot of pretty kids. Let me see, she had Perley, Lucille, Margie and Violette. Aunt Perley just had Sylvia. Violet never had any children. Margie had Wellford and a daughter that passed away. Lucille had four or five children, Sharon, Kenneth, Wendell, and um, I lost a lot of my memory. Since I got COVID-19, I don't remember things like I used to."

There was a crow on a branch who seemed to have joined the conversation in the background and she was screaming at him telling him to shhhhh.

Sierra - "So, what's your favorite memory of your uncle?"

Barbara - "Oh, I love my uncle. I remember one time, he came up to Chicago..." She said and started giggling. "I had a bed, and threw him off it in the middle of the night, then I heard him fussing and cussing. He said it was like a bucking bull. I love my uncle for that, he complained about my bed every time he saw me. When I was living on Bay St southeast, my father got sick, so I had to sell that house. When he would come to visit, he would sit with my dad. They both were in the army.

LET'S TALK ABOUT DEATH, CAN WE?

He was always nice to us. He would take us out to eat and stuff. We always had a great time with him and your grandmother. Your grandmother was a very nice woman. Your granddad would visit when I lived on Bay Street. He would sit down on the front porch with my father and they would talk about the old times.

Their father was an Indian man that lived in the mountains. An Aztec Indian, I believe I'm saying it correctly."

She was now finished with the task at hand, so she said, "Let's go in." Since I was closer to the door I tried to open it but it was locked.

Barbara - "I guess Beeves forgot to unlock the back door, or he didn't hear me."

I offered to go around and do it so she wouldn't have to get her feet dirty. She declined and so we walked around to the front together. I'm excited about going in because she's always feeding me something. The last time I was over she fixed me this bread-type stuff and cheese. I don't recall what she said it was by name although, once tasting it, my food memory kicked in.

Not sure if that is a thing but what I'm saying is that my taste buds definitely remembered having this before. This was certainly a Belizean thing, but all I know is it was causing me great joy to be experiencing this moment. I do also remember going to the house on Bay Street that she mentioned. Either with my granddaddy or Patti. It was a big nice house, I don't remember the color it was or anything but I do remember the front yard looking and feeling much like her back yard at this house, peaceful and serene.

Chapter 16

DADDY'S GIRL

Chantay D. Burgess, February 27, 1961 – August 8, 2013

This interview was different than the others. The others brought me unspeakable joy, but to be interviewing my mother about her father felt like an honor. I was a little nervous in doing it honestly, but hey, I'm a reporter, remember? We never run away from a good story. Plus, the little girl in me was so ready to hear about my mother's childhood experiences.

I started off the questioning with, "Ok, so tell me about your daddy."

Duke - "Why do you want to know about my daddy?" She asked with a straight face and serious tone before continuing, "My daddy was a daddy."

Sierra - I chuckled and repeated, "Your daddy was a daddy?"

Duke - "Yeah, my daddy was a daddy. My daddy was a good man. He had his faults like every typical man did, but he never strayed away from us. My daddy was a good daddy," She emphasized with this little girl's smile on her face. "He never made us feel like we weren't a priority. He was always there. We used to go to church on Sunday. Mama would send us to church with Dad."

I interrupted her and said, "So Grandma would send y'all?"

Duke - "Grandma didn't go, no. Grandma was home cooking Sunday dinner so we went to church with Dad." She laughed again and said, "The church's name was Travels Rest. It was somewhere off of 16th Street. Back then we lived in Laurel Park, no correction, I'm not sure where we lived at. The tree wasn't too far from the house."

Sierra - "What tree?"

Duke - "The tree that dad used to go and hang out at after church. With the fellas Mom used to look for us to come home and we were under the tree."

Sierra - "In your church dresses?"

Duke - "Yes sir, yes, in our church dresses, looking sharp as a tack. He used to go have him a little drink with the fellas, before he went home. He never had more than two beers. Dad would then put us in the car and we would go home. When we got home, we would change our clothes and go outside to play until it was time for dinner. Like I said, he was always there for us. He was a good dad."

I love the fact that she kept repeating that statement with this little girl smile on her face

Duke - "He made sure we had food on the table and clothes on our backs. He also made sure we were respectable. What else do you want to know about dad?"

She said this like there was a problem. I wasn't questioning her about whether her father was a good father, I was simply trying to get to know information about my granddad.

Sierra - "So when I say Royal Court, what does that mean to you?"

Duke - "Oh, Royal Court! That's where we grew up. We were little then, it was kind of a rough neighborhood, like the projects."

Sierra - "So Royal Court was the projects?"

Duke - "Yes, nothing but bay-bay kids."

Sierra - "Bay-bay kids?" I repeated. I haven't heard this term in so long

Duke - "Yes, bay-bay kids. Although we weren't bay-bay kids, we lived in a neighborhood with the bay-bay kids. Everybody loved everybody in the neighborhood. Everybody loved Mom and Dad."

She painted a picture of everybody playing together in the neighborhood.

Duke - "It wasn't the crap going on in neighborhoods today where there's a division but everybody got along very well. Kids were being kids, we had a great time. That's about all I can tell you about Royal Court. What else do you want to know?"

Sierra - "Where do you remember your father working when you were younger?"

She leaned back in her chair as if to prepare for the ride down memory lane.

Duke - "Let me think about it…where did he work? He worked at the city in sanitation garbage. Dad was a garbage man. He would come home every day smelling like garbage, but Elnora wasn't playing that he wasn't coming up in her house smelling like garbage…not Elnora. She didn't play that, shirt, shoes, and socks came off at the front door.

He was lucky if she put a washcloth and towel on the outside, either way, he was not coming up in there smelling like that. Elnora wasn't having it! We used to like that when we were little, we made a game out of it. We used to get to play in the water when Dad came home. Everybody in the neighborhood would come because we could play in the water hose while Dad was washing off. I had a great childhood, a great childhood," she repeated. "I don't remember too many bad things, I mostly had a great childhood."

Sierra - "Did granddad cook food from his country back home in Belize?"

Duke - "I do remember he would make this lemon meringue pie, not the fake stuff, but with real condensed milk. It wasn't like the crap that they use today. You also take real lemons, squeeze them, and you keep mixing to bond the milk with the lemon juice, You have to be patient when making this.

He also used to do this stuff with this corn and cornbread. It crunched so good. I'm not sure what he used to do to it, but it was so good. Don't be trying to get any family secrets out of me because I'm not giving you any. We cooked together from time to time, but he didn't do too much cooking; he didn't play that kitchen stuff much.

Dad did the work, so he didn't do a lot of cooking. He made sure all the bills were paid, the clothes were clean, and everybody went to school. I even learned how to do hair because I was responsible for braiding everyone's hair. My sisters had a brand-new hairstyle every week, everyone always wondered who did their hair but it was me. I did that."

Although I'm on a mystery to uncover the secrets of my grandfather's life, I also wanted to get the tea

Sierra - "So, tell me your side of the story about the day grandmother drove the station wagon up to the bar where granddaddy was."

She crossed her hands over her belly and tapped her feet a little. She let out another long sigh as if she was taken to another place and time.

Duke - "You're talking about, the bar on 3rd Avenue. Listen...there was a little juke joint on 3rd Avenue where dad used to hang out a lot. He just went there to hang out and kick back a little bit, but he came home every day. It doesn't matter, he came home and went out every now and then.

I was about 9 or 10, Patti was about 6. Mommy loaded that station wagon up with all of dad's stuff and put us in the car. She had us all cramped in the back seat but we made it. Yes sir, drove Betsy straight to 3rd Ave. Cozy Corner."

Sierra - "What color was the station wagon?"

Duke - "Brown."

I can remember there being a brown and tan station wagon in the driveway.

Sierra - "How did you know where you were going?"

Duke - "We had made that drive before. This was the first time his clothes came with us. She took us up there and told us to get his things out of her car."

Sierra - "So I wonder why she felt the need to take y'all with her? Repeating get his stuff out my car…again."

Duke - "Poor man."

Sierra - "So she made his kids take his stuff out of the car?"

Duke - "When we got there, Momma got out of the car, and went in the bar. She came back with Hugh Burgess' keys, opened the doors, and told us to get his things out of her car. When we were finished, she returned his keys and we left."

Perhaps Duke could see the shocked look on my face as she said quickly, "It wasn't a fight or nothing like that."

Sierra - "What house was this at? Did ya'll live on Union St?"

Duke - "Yes, we lived on Union St at the time."

Sierra - "Was that the last time he came home?"

Duke - "No, he came back after that. That night, he slept in the driveway. Maybe the next day she let him back in but he didn't stay this time, he left. He left cause he got tired of Mom coming up there with the bull crap. Elnora was no joke.

But I had a good childhood. We lived in a good neighborhood. I remember we used to go down to Lake Margorie at night before they fenced it off. There were gators down there, but they didn't bother us. We were kids, we were always down there. We did everything down there. It was nice."

Sierra, thinking to myself, kids are the perfect snack. "No ma, I don't think it was because y'all were kids."

Duke - "I remember one time when Patti got the measles. But yeah, she got the measles and they went back in her or something. Patti couldn't walk, I'll get Wanda to tell you the story. I can't forget because we had to carry her little fat butt everywhere."

You could see her holding back her laugh and smile.

Sierra - "Well, where did she need to go that y'all had to tote her?"

Duke - "Everywhere! Everywhere we went, she felt she had to go too."

Sierra - "So wait, how did y'all not catch it?"

Duke - "She was late getting the chickenpox so it affected her differently. She got sick and couldn't walk. She would cry and cry, and Momma made us take her with us. I think Wanda got her drunk and she started walking. I don't know exactly what happened, but she finally started walking again. She needed to, I was tired of carrying her fat butt. That is the only incident I remember from back then. I'm telling you I had a good childhood. We used to walk all the way to Southside to get to school."

Sierra - "Southside Fundamental, that's off 9th Street. What grade was this?"

Duke - "Yeah, off 9th Street. We used to walk all the way there and back. I was in the sixth, seventh, eighth, or ninth grade. Whatever grade it was, I don't remember. Southside, that's where I got my name Duke, well the people in school called me by it, but dad gave me that name when I was younger. Do you remember those black doodlebugs? And the T.V show with John Wayne and the Duke? So, from that combo, it's the name my dad decided to give me. It stuck with me throughout school.

I was the good guy in school despite my reputation of being the bad girl. When bullies used to tease other children because they were less fortunate, I didn't like that. I would stand up for them. You don't have a job, you don't buy no clothes. Your momma ain't no better than theirs…"

She was ranting as if she was speaking up for them even now.

I was trying to get my two cents in but she kept on ranting.

Duke - "And so it made me the bad girl. I wasn't the bad guy, even though I could fight and beat a lot of asses. I only beat up people for those who couldn't defend themselves. I never fought the girls because they were no match for me."

Sierra - "They weren't any competition?"

Duke - "No sir, they didn't know enough."

I chuckled under my breath as she continued.

Duke - "See my dad was a boxer. He taught us a lot when we were little. We could get on the roof to fix shingles with a staple gun. And although we were girls, dad taught us everything. Desmond was the only boy and Dad didn't discriminate. He taught us everything he taught my brother.

The bottom line was, I didn't fight girls. All in all, they didn't know enough to beat me. Don't make me hurt you, you know what I'm saying."

That is why you hear Joe always saying that she didn't fight anyone but guys. Joe is a gentleman that she went to school with who knows firsthand about this story she's telling. I had the opportunity to hear it straight from his mouth. One day, me and Auntie Patti decided to go to lunch, and he was in the parking lot of the restaurant telling me all about it. Joe said once my mom graduated from school, she let all the boys know not to try to get in a relationship with her little sister. He also told me how she had all the guys at the school scared of her, so much so that they created a call so if she was seen coming down the hallway, they would echo it out loud and the other guys knew to run.

Duke - "Fighting the girls was too easy but the boys helped me perfect my craft."

Sierra - "Oh, so they challenged you."

Duke - "Yes, fighting with guys taught me a lot. You know I'm saying I was able to take a punch, come on. If you can't take a punch, guess what? You're in trouble."

Sierra - "Ooooh ok."

Duke - "You got to be able to take a punch, man. People knew not to mess with us."

I don't think it's any coincidence that my mother too was the protector of others from bullies. I also defended people from being picked on in school for what they didn't have. It's so heartfelt to know that we are so much more alike than I was led to believe and not in my heart, but by people who only talked about my mother for the condition she had, not the position that she held. 'Ain't a woman alive that can take my mom's place,' I thought in Tupac's voice.

And, so Duke stuck with me through middle school and high school.

Sierra - "Tell me your favorite memory of your father."

I have to say, I love the way my mom says, dad. You can hear the love she has for him. She lets out a giggle at my last question.

Duke - "My favorite memory was every 4th of July or Memorial Day, it didn't matter what holiday. He would have us up at the crack of dawn. We would pack the car with food and supplies for the day. We went to Clearwater or Sarasota, somewhere with nice water. No barnacles or a bunch of seaweed, no stinky ocean smell. We had picnics. It was family time; dad was really big on this. Those were my best memories."

It's funny that she said this because this was actually one of the phenomenal things that I remember. My grandfather and the family picnics with all my little cousins under the oak tree in the yard of the big red brick house.

Duke - "We always had a good time. He taught us how to swim. I remember his hair curling up instantly the moment it got wet. Dad was a wonderful swimmer."

Sierra - "Do you remember Lake City? What are your memories about it? It's where Grandma came from and you were born at Bayfront, right?

Duke - "Grandma was from Lake City, Jacksonville area. I do remember them taking us up that way. They were really slick, they got me the first time they drove us to Lake City. It's a two-way road, you don't see nothing but railroad tracks with houses on the other side. I was a city kid. Listen, city kids never see chickens running around. I had never slapped a hog. These people…"

Sierra, interrupting - "Are you talking about your mother and father?"

Duke - "Yes, those two, Hugh and Elnora. They drove us to Lake City, introduced us to a lady then had us unload the car. At that moment, I had no idea it was our stuff they took out the car and before I knew it, they were gone. Then year after year, they just got sneakier and sneakier. I thought we were just taking a ride and lo and behold, we ended up in Lake City."

Sierra - "So who was this lady? It wasn't your grandmother?"

Duke - "They said to call her grandmother but I am uncertain to which grandmother. I don't know if it was dad's mom or mom's mom."

Sierra - "And this was country?" I asked, laughing. She's so comical, I see where I get my sense of humor from, my mother is a riot.

They had the city girl in the country.

Duke - "Listen...we had an outhouse! Although there was a bathroom on the inside but when we were outside playing, we used the outhouse because she wasn't going for us running in and out of her house. When I tell you it was the country. I remember she sent us to the store one time and I promised it felt like it was a 150-mile walk."

Sierra - "What did y'all have to go get, do you remember?"

Duke - "No, I don't remember. All I know is we had to go to the store and it was 150 miles away. I remember some of my cousins being there. They were older, like 15 and 16, and Grandma would let us hang out with them sometimes. They took us out to the club one time to a party in a barn. It seemed like it was going to fall down. They were out there having a good time, the whole house was rocking."

Sierra - "So you had a good time."

Duke - "Girl...Listen, I was in the corner scared for my life."

Sierra - "Sounds like it was made out of wood."

Duke - "Man, I was in the corner praying that the floor didn't fall in. But all in all, everybody had a good time. I was so glad to get out of there and we had to walk those 150 miles all the way back home. Seemed like no matter where you went in the country, it was 150 miles away.

I was a city girl, so by the time I did all that walking, wasn't nobody trying to dance. My legs hurt. They were used to it because they walked all the time because they were country folks and I was a city girl.

I remember one time, Grandma sent me out there to go catch a chicken. If I remember correctly, I think I took a rock and bust the chicken in the head because that was the way this city girl was going to kill the chicken.

Grandma did try to teach me that if you wrap your hands around the chicken's neck a certain way, you could just snap it. Grandma's house was made from wood too, but it didn't creep like that barn party. You could tell that it was unleveled. The kitchen was stable and stuff, we slept good, we ate good, it's just that it was the country. It was unfamiliar and everything you needed to do or wanted to go do was 150 miles away. At least that's what it seemed like.

Wanda was born in the country somewhere from what I understand. The story that I was told was Wanda was born in the house by a midwife, I don't know what mama was doing back then. But the story is, Wanda was born with a veil over her face. Now, that's something you can research if you like. I seen this veil for myself, with my own eyes. Now, I wasn't born yet, so I didn't see Wanda being born with a spider web thing over her face. I just know they had to pull it off of her. I heard the stories of they put it in the jar and put it in a special solution.

But, when we moved to Florida, I remember one time when I was in Mama's room and I found the jar. This spider web, veil thing was on the inside of it. As time passed, I'm unsure of how much time went by actually. Momma had moved it and I discovered it again in her room and it had disappeared. It was no longer there, for it seemed to have evaporated. I would say it dissolved within the solution because the jar was still there, but not the spider web. This is why we call Wanda nuts because of that thing that she was born with over her face."

Sierra, switching up the subject as I bring the interview to an end - "What high school did you graduate from?"

Duke - "Bogey Ciega."

Sierra - "Did you play sports? What did you do for fun?"

Duke - "I played tennis."

Sierra - "What! I didn't know you played tennis."

Duke - "I loved to play tennis. Boy, I had an ace out of this world. Damn y'all, I had so much power behind that forehand, plus I had thick legs."

Sierra - "What did you do for fun?"

Duke - "We also played at Bear Pool Room which used to be on 18th avenue. If you look it up, you might be able to find some pictures somewhere. We played softball at Bear's Pool Room as they had a softball league. Me, Wanda, Patty, all of us. You might find some pictures of us playing softball."

Sierra - "What was the name of the team?"

Duke - "I don't remember the name of the team. But I also liked to play pool. My brother was a pool shark so I learned all I knew from him. He also had a race car so he would race with other people. They called him the mad Nova."

Sierra - "Wait, so which brother had the race car?"

Duke - "Desmond."

Sierra - "I didn't know Uncle Desmond played pool too. I thought it was only Uncle Larry. You know they both knew how to play pool and did it very well."

Duke - "Everything was good back then. You see what I'm saying? Everybody was family, we had good communication, but since everyone has grown up, they've distanced themselves now. Life pulls you in different directions."

Sierra - "Tell me about your experience with segregation."

Duke - "With what?"

Sierra - "Segregation is when they had the white people and the black people separated."

Duke - "Oh ok...Boca Ciega was the first school that they desegregated out there in Gulfport. Listen, those white folks told us black folks that they didn't want us out there at a certain time, and they meant it. They used to run us all the way up that road from Boca Ciega High School until you get across the street."

Sierra - "Across what street...49th Street?"

Duke - "Yep, they ran your ass all the way to 49th Street."

Sierra - "Wait, so kids from the school? Kids your age were running after you? Was it adults?"

Duke - "It could be one or the other but some days it was both. I remember one time, we were having a session in class and this girl sat in front of me who had long hair. She used to intentionally flip her hair and hit me in the face with it because I sat directly behind her."

Sierra, letting out a chuckle - "What color was it?"

Duke - "Blonde and brown. She intentionally would do this and she would play with her hair all day flipping it back on me. In one part of the school, they started a riot. The teacher told us to take our seats and tried to lock us in the classroom to keep us safe. At some point, something popped off in the classroom and we started to riot inside. I just so happened to have a pair of scissors on this particular day and I cut her damn hair. Everybody started fighting in the classroom. At some point, the classroom door opened and we all made a run for it. She was out of hair, and I was gone."

The picture is becoming clearer and clearer as I interview others. Their words add color to the picture which brings it to life. Duke said she was at Bogie, I remember when talking to Auntie Wanda she said she graduated from Lakewood. So, I asked Mom how everybody went to a different school.

Duke - "Wanda was a bit older so she went to a different school because she was in high school, and we were still in middle school and under. But it also had to do with the de-segregation of everything at that point to keep a certain number of colors and whites in the school to show the balance and coming together of the two races.

But, they ran us clear to 49th Street every chance they could get. We were not to be over there on that side of the town after a certain time and they made it clear they didn't want us over there.

I remember there was this store that we used to go to that was on the corner, but it's closed now. They had this wine in there that we used to drink. Wait, I think the name of it was Mad Dog."

With great excitement, I chimed in and finished the statement by saying, "20/20," because I knew exactly what she was talking about. I just find it humorous how some of the things my mother did or endured were reflected in some of the actions that I lived out. For example, going to the store and buying Mad Dog 20/20 was a part of my middle school and high school experience.

Sierra - "What was your favorite flavor?"

Duke - "I don't know. Nobody was drinking for flavor, you were drinking to get tipsy. That's all we cared about back then.

Some might want to argue that it was not a black or a white thing and that would be easy for them to say since they weren't the ones running for their lives with a crowd of white people chasing behind them. I'm just answering your question with accurate and true information from the experience that I had of being a colored girl in a newly desegregated school.

And even though the law was put in place for us to come together, white people only abided when in school. Because when school was over, there was no hesitation from them showing how they still truly felt towards children that looked like me in certain parts of town.

Being disliked for the color of your skin was still going on in 1971. Even though there were rules and catchy slogans like, 'Can't we all just get along?' in the years to follow. Fast forward to the current day, the color of my skin is still offensive to some. What I speak of is still present in some areas."

What do you have a taste for?

How much could knowing where you come from add color to your life? How much would taking a bite of your family tree alter your palate? Change your narrative of the life you are currently living? Disrupt the way you do and see things?

One thing I did know, as I found myself chewing on these very same questions was that by no means does my journey stop here! I'd love to implore you as the reader to reflect on your history as well. Perhaps your knowledge of these things will create an appetite for knowledge.

While on this rooted journey, I found the purpose of wanting to know more about my history. The reason for this much-needed collision was not to point blame but to examine the stories of the old, which created this hunger. To use it not to apply it, but to learn from it and do better because of it. This has become more than just my history. I now see that learned history will be your story you'll leave behind for others to expand upon to ensure we are not making the same mistakes, repeating the same cycles, and overlooking what no longer works.

And that precisely is my responsibility and yours to do individually, as a collective, and (as a whole) for our world to be a better place for all that exists on this planet, creating new beginnings and a new perspective.

My identity is a manifestation of my experiences, the people, places, and things that I've encountered. Not because it happened, but for the clarity it provided. The person (character) I am was up to me. The stories that are left behind that we call history arms us with information that we all have a choice to use as knowledge to empower us or allow it to be shadows of the past that may haunt us.

The way to ensure that we are no longer waiting on the change to come is to be the change we want to see in human affairs and the ways this will affect, influence or determine the unlearned patterns in our society. We don't perish for the lack of knowledge, we perish from not using the knowledge. Applied knowledge is power, the brain is our strongest muscle.

History nor this book alone will not change your life. How you use what you find in it will. Using that power to redefine what it means to be you, what it means to be an American, and what it now means to be (copper-colored) black.

Savor the flavors of this fine dining experience. Oh, taste and see, that it's disrupting mindsets that welcome present developments, clarity on living a life well-lived, and future hopes.

It's time, it's time, the time is NOW to be the change. We are the people that can do it. If we don't know what our future world will look like, we have to be intentional with our life stories that we leave behind.

Where are you heading? On this teacher's journey called life? If the page you are currently living is the one to tell your story, are you happy with it? If the mindset you currently have was used to help someone understand your past, what would you be passing down to them? The future can and will only be as bright as we make it today!

"Those who have no record of what their forebears have accomplished lose the inspiration which comes from the teaching of biography and history."
- *Dr. Carter G. Woodson*

Putting these words on paper is my promissory note to the future that I will play my part to ensure I don't just dream, but I dream OUT LOUD. My life and this book's mission is to make sure our present day, the youth, and the world at large have examples (this is the out loud) of what oppression transformed into an oasis of freedom and justice looks like. The example of what it feels like to live in a nation where they will not be judged by the color of their skin but by the content of their character.

The out loud example of making every valley exalted and all crooked paths made straight. These are some of the words Martin Luther King spoke in 1963. Here today the year is 2021 and although some things have changed, sadly, much remains the same. Martin Luther King had a dream, now I ask for the sake of copper-colored little boys and girls, for the sake of justice being for all God's creations, that we no longer just dream, but (be the example) DREAM OUT LOUD.

ABOUT THE AUTHOR

Sierra M. Clark was born in St. Petersburg Florida and is the bloodline of her Belizean Grandfather. She's a Motivational Exhorter, Heart Coach, and Author. She has spent most of her life caring for others but loves what she does. She has over 20 years of experience in healthcare, which she calls hearting it forward. She's honored to say that she has been a CNA, HHA, and currently, a Patient Care Tech at her local children's hospital.

Sierra has packaged her experiences, passion, and her ability to hear hearts into her Exhortation Program, stimulating and transforming hearts.

Sierra has been someone who others could easily open up to and share their troubles. She has also been the one people come to for guidance in their life's journey. Even as a child, people would seek her out for advice and she knows that she was created to give and reflect love while building others up.

Sierra Clark is on a journey to see her internal beauty and be her purpose in life. She wants to bring love to the planet and find color in the everyday. She invites you to join her along the path of spiritual awakening to uncover joyfulness and the life you deserve.

Sierra Clark is also the founder of Transformation AcadeME, a program designed to help others master the heart and heighten their levels of self-communication. She aims to target the self-limitations people believe and place on themselves.

SIERRA CLARK

has had the gift of being someone people can talk to as far back as she can remember. She's been the voice of reason for many, and it seems even at a young age, people valued her two cents.

In 42 years, she's never met a stranger. Yep, she's the person random people find comfort in talking to in the line at the grocery store.

Is it her laughter that's calming and explosive all at the same time? Perhaps it's her magnetic personality that draws you in like your favorite movie. Could it be her illuminating smile that feels like sunshine? Or the warmth of her soul that comforts you like a slice of grandma's warm apple pie?

Some might say she has a gift, or even call it an anointing. Either way there is no question as to why she's been invited to speak in pool pits around her city. She finds great joy in mentoring at a few local high schools and elementary schools.

There is no reason to wonder why, when doing speaking engagements, she connects with the audience. Whether if it's in a class room, a women's retreat with a room of 500+ women or something more intimate like in a local park with a small group of people.

Sierra hears the hearts of people, she credits that to her super power, she takes that saying, "Put yourself, in my shoes," literally.

Sierra finds joy in doing unto others as she would do unto herself. So, she delivers as if she too was sitting in the audience and needed the message herself.

CONTACT SIERRA:

✉ INFO@SIERRACLARK.LIFE

🌐 SIERRACLARK.LIFE

CALL TO ACTION

Want to know what Sierra was doing before she became an Author?

Here's a link to some footage, where you can hear and see for yourself.

https://youtube.com/channel/UCijXE0SFgEFp13WJY8N4ZcQ

Watch, Download, Share

www.ingramcontent.com/pod-product-compliance
Lightning Source LLC
Chambersburg PA
CBHW030039100526
44590CB00011B/264